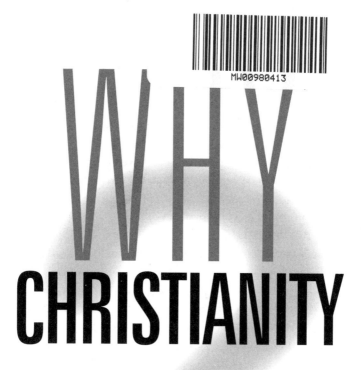

WHY
CHRISTIANITY
?

A A HALL

CREATION
HOUSE
A STRANG COMPANY

WHY CHRISTIANITY? by Al A. Hall
Published by Creation House
A Strang Company
600 Rinehart Road
Lake Mary, Florida 32746
www.creationhouse.com

Unless otherwise noted, Scripture quotations are from the Holy Bible, New International Version of the Bible. Copyright © 1973, 1978, 1984, International Bible Society. Used by permission.

Scripture quotations marked ASV are from the American Standard Bible. Copyright © 1960, 1962, 1968, 1971, 1972, 1973, 1975, by the Lockman Foundation. Used by permission.

Scripture quotations marked KJV are from the King James Version of the Bible.

Scripture quotations marked NKJV are from the New King James Version of the Bible. Copyright © 1979, 1980, 1982 by Thomas Nelson, Inc., publishers. Used by permission.

Scripture quotations marked NRSV are from the New Revised Standard Version of the Bible. Copyright © 1989 by the Division of Christian Education of the National Council of the Churches of Christ in the USA. Used by permission.

Scripture quotations marked ISV are from the *Holy Bible: International Standard Version*. Copyright © 1996–2008 by the ISV Foundation. All rights reserved internationally. Used by permission.

Scripture quotations marked DNT are from The Holy Bible: Darby's New Translation, 1961.

Scripture quotations marked YLT are from Young's Literal Translations by Robert Young, 1898.

Unless otherwise noted, all definitions are from *Merriam-Webster's Collegiate Dictionary, 11th ed.* (Springfield, MA: Merriam-Webster Inc., 2006).

Publisher's Note: The views expressed in this book are not necessarily the views held by the publisher.

Design Director: Bill Johnson
Cover design by Karen Grindley

Library of Congress Control Number: 2008936178
International Standard Book Number: 978-1-59979-483-9

First Edition

08 09 10 11 12 — 987654321
Printed in the United States of America

CONTENTS

?

PREFACE

THIS BOOK IS for Christians as well as those who desire to understand the fundamental beliefs of Christianity. Its purpose is to help Christians understand their unique relationship with God. To a non-Christian it is a strange or difficult concept to understand. Many people believe in a god. However, non-Christians will usually believe that God has criteria or standards of behavior that must be followed in order to please Him and be saved from hell. They believe that after their death, they will be judged, usually with either a simple concept of balancing the "good" versus "bad" of their life or through the implementation of appropriate sacrifices meant to offset their sins. Christianity is completely different because it recognizes that God no longer has a merit system for judging man's behavior. Instead, judgment concerns the purity of one's spirit, because either our spirit will spend an eternity in a relationship with God or we shall be out of His presence for all eternity.

There is only one way to achieve the necessary purity of spirit, and that is for God to cleanse our spirit of sin. The only way to accomplish this involves Jesus' indwelling Spirit joining our spirit and abiding within us while we are alive. This can only occur when Jesus is invited into our heart. However, before that can occur, there must exist faith that God exists and that He became flesh, in the person of Jesus, who died as the atonement or sacrifice for our sin. What is even more amazing is that Jesus, while in the person of God, created all things knowing that He would then temporarily limit Himself by indwelling a human body to become the sacrifice needed for man's salvation. The sacrifice of His sinless human existence—by death caused by religious men—was to reconcile all He created to Himself by becoming the only atonement for the sin of all mankind who, by faith, believe in Him and invite His Spirit within them.

Sin, with the negative consequences it has on one's relationship with God, is the inevitable result for humanity because of an individual's exercise of free will. Sin must be eliminated from a man's spirit before he is able to join God in an eternal spiritual existence. As Christians, we recognize that God's sacrifice was not a general pardon of all humanity, but an opportunity for those who believe and have faith in Jesus, the Son of God.

For various reasons, man will continue to sin even after becoming a Christian. Christianity is unique, however, because it involves a relationship with Jesus by our spirit, which becomes an experience that continues to change us and clean us of sin throughout the rest of our lives. The goal is to conform us into the likeness of Jesus. As an added dimension to our relationship, Jesus has also given us the Holy Spirit to help guide us toward that goal. To help us mature, there are certain concepts all Christians need to understand.

First, you need to understand the Trinity and the reason for Jesus' sacrifice. Second, but related to the first concept, you need to understand the difference phases man has experienced in his relationship with God and why we are presently in an era of faith with Jesus. Third, you need to understand basic beliefs of Christianity so you will not be diverted from the truth. Fourth, you need to understand that salvation is not the only experience awaiting you. There is also the baptism with the Holy Spirit and with fire, which is the sanctification of your spirit. Finally, you need to understand current misconceptions that are subtly attacking Christianity so you are not deceived into diluting New Testament principles of faith with "laws" from the Old Testament covenant.

My desire is that this book will provide insight concerning Christianity and encourage you in your walk with Jesus on your path of sanctification so that you can accomplish Paul's challenge in Ephesians 4:12–15:

> That the body of Christ may be built up until we all reach unity in the faith and knowledge of the Son of God and become mature, attaining to the whole measure of the fullness of Christ. Then we will no longer be infants, tossed back and forth by the waves, and blown here and there by every wind of teaching and by the cunning and craftiness of men in their deceitful scheming. Instead, speaking the truth in love, we will in all things grow up into Him who is the Head, that is, Christ.

This book covers the basics that all Christians should understand. Foremost, it will help you understand that we are in an age or era of faith, which was the reason for all creation. As such, you will understand the differences between fleshly works, even though they may appear to be desirable, and those that come from your spirit. The fundamentals contained in this book are also intended to free you from the bondage created by religious men. The very same spirits that killed Jesus want to put you into the bondage from which Jesus freed us almost two thousand years ago. In addition, there is a discussion on non-biblical ideas by some Christian leaders attempting to determine when and how Jesus will return at the end of the age.

I wish to thank Pastor Sam Lalaian at The Dwelling Place church of Loganville, Georgia, for his insightful review.

INTRODUCTION
Man's Dilemma

OR CENTURIES, MAN has believed that a God existed. Since then, he has also thought that there had to be a way of pleasing God and being accepted by Him. Man has also believed that it was his actions that were the criteria that God would use in measuring an individual's acceptance or rejection.

There were—and still are today—three basic concepts that man has believed about his relationship to God. The first is that man's good and bad deeds would be weighed against each other on a balance scale; and if the good outweighed the bad, he would be approved by God after his death. A second concept is that if one wanted to aid or increase the weight of the good deeds, the bad deeds needed to be expunged by making a suitable sacrifice to God, leaving only the good deeds to be judged and thus insuring a reward from God. The third concept, a variation on the other two, recognizes that bad deeds need to be prevented. This involves learning rules and laws that train or condition man so that he doesn't do the bad deeds or that when he does, sacrifices can be made for it.

A major problem, however, is that under each of these concepts, man is in bondage to a system of rules and religious laws that control his actions. Christianity is just the opposite.

The problem with all of these concepts is that they ignore the spirit of a man and merely address the spirit when it is expressed through man's actions, not its true condition, which is often hidden from exposure. God, however, being pure Spirit, looks upon a man's spirit and judges its purity. For centuries man did not understand that a man's spirit cannot be changed by externals, in other words, by controlling the flesh. God, however, can change a man's spirit. This is achieved through His Son, Jesus Christ. Among other things, this book will explain God's plan for man's spirit to be reborn and how to enter into a relationship with God that grows and matures.

1

CAN WE REALLY KNOW GOD?

Yes, we can.

And other than the wonders of Creation, proof of God only becomes clear after a rebirth of your spirit.[1] *Rebirth* means that a "new" spirit opens the door into a spiritual realm where there is an interaction or relationship with God. As Christians, we begin to experience and come to know God. This relationship only occurs with Christians. Faith in the true God is extremely important. Your belief, hope, and expectations must have their focus on the truth, not a counterfeit created by Satan who spreads misconceptions and lies. The place of your eternal existence after the death of your physical body depends on this. God planned this before the beginning of time, and He sent Jesus to create the opportunity for humanity to know God. Satan has sent counterfeits with the intention of misleading you toward a path of a belief in a false god.[2]

The rebirth of your spirit does not occur by merely believing that God exists and attempting to follow certain prescribed religious standards of conduct. Rebirth is not achieved by training or controlling your actions, or even by following established rituals dictated by a religion; in other words, using or following what are termed religious "rules" to justify your belief that you are worthy of acceptance by God.[3] These are merely fleshly acts that do not affect your inner self or spirit in a positive way.

Only a rebirth of your spirit, which you might not even recognize has occurred and which is the cleansing of your spirit of sin, allows you to move into a relationship with God. Until that happens, you cannot actually have a

---

1 An intellectual determination concerning the existence of God is futile. That determination can only be made by your spirit, or heart, where God has planted the seed of belief. If allowed to grow, God will reveal Himself. However, Satan will also attempt to hinder that growth by creating a lie about who God really is, namely, that God is a demanding and judgmental God. Satan specifically does not want you to believe that God loves you.

2 Satan confuses the minds of men with deception and causes them to believe in his fabrications. Thus, Satan uses man's earnest desires for God to cause them to be delusional. Then, with what they believe are good intentions, men spread Satan's lies to others, creating a false concept of God and false methods of pleasing God.

3 Many religions have, as a basis, the belief that God exists. Under those religious systems, man attempts to live according to the rules the founders of the religious system believed would please God. Christianity has as its basic belief the concept that a relationship between man and God can be created beginning with a rebirth of our spirit, which is the result of the belief and faith in Jesus. This is a unique situation that sets Christianity apart from religious systems. The depth or breath of the relationship varies depending on many factors, including the beliefs and principles indicated in this book.

relationship with God. In addition, nothing you do, other than accepting and believing in your heart that Jesus, who was and is the Son of God who sacrificed Himself as a sin offering to God for us, can cause your spirit to be reborn.

It is God who proves Himself; one cannot prove God. However, unless you want to wait until you are being judged—for we all will be judged—and found wanting because of the sin within your spirit, there really is no other way that allows God to prove Himself, except through your acceptance in your heart or spirit of Jesus. Prior to that acceptance, He will not abide in you. Only you can open the "door" into your heart, and you must actively invite Him into your heart.

From a historical perspective, it is important to understand that angels were created before man. They had free will, but approximately one-third chose to follow or side with a rebellious angel by the name of Lucifer (Satan) in a challenge against God. What was the difference between those angels and the ones who did not rebel? It was faith in God. Thus, faith in Jesus is the door through which God is invited into your heart. There is no other way, because along with faith there is also trust. If the angels who followed Lucifer had faith and trust in God, they never would have followed Lucifer. The majority of angels loved and trusted God above all else, and they were not fooled or lulled into believing Satan's justification for rebellion. Consequently, like the angels, faith also is required of us. No laws or rules that merely have the effect of shaping your behavior are sufficient because your spirit can still be in rebellion and full of pride.[4] The religions man has created fail to understand this requirement of faith (not to be confused with belief) in God and the fact that the use of religious acts as their means of access to God is ineffective. However, they also fail because they confuse their beliefs with true faith that can only be achieved through Jesus.[5]

---

4 Often the rebellion is not directly confrontational against God, but it is focused upon self. Thus, pride is present when self is first in your heart.

5 The concept of the Trinity, discussed below, is very important. Its basis is a recognition that Jesus, aka the Word, told the truth that He was with the Father prior to coming to Earth in the incarnate form of a man, who used, and still uses, the name Jesus. It appears difficult for some people to deal with the concept that God may be composed of three individual parts, which is called the Trinity, consisting of the Father, the Son (Jesus), and the Holy Spirit. However, is there any reason why God's form or existence is limited to any particular form imagined by man? He is One God. Not only one in purpose, and one in unity, but also a composite entity that had the capability to separate Himself to carry out His purposes relating to creation, and eternity. How can man's limited intellect fully understand God, moreover, set himself up as a judge of God's capabilities? When man does this, basically rejecting what Jesus said, he deceives himself into thinking he can define God better than God defines Himself. Rejecting the concept of the Trinity has severe consequences that will be explained later in this book.

Christianity—faith in Jesus—is a reflection of the freedom God wants us to have. The free will to make choices is paramount to God.[6] Primarily, God is a God of love, not punishment. He has proven this attribute because He gave of Himself, His Son, to be the atonement for our sin if we accept, believe, and have faith in Him. In other words, God demonstrated His love when He gave His physical life, Jesus, for us. Thus, because of God's love, we have the free will choice to accept Him or reject Him. However, everything our spirit needs is in Jesus. In fact, the totality of God is expressed by and through Jesus.[7] We must remove the barriers and open our spirit to Him.

Because we exercise our free will in order for faith to exist, God does not compel people.[8] If He did, there would be no freedom of choice. Without freedom of choice, there would be no love, merely obedience. In that situation, you would be like a pet, subject to discipline and rewards. With adequate training, our actions would be controlled, but our love would be nonexistent or conditional. In fact, our spirits would be angry but repressed because of the fear of punishment. There can never be a relationship with God when you are not free to make choices.

Generally, it can be said that every religion except for Christianity has as its core belief that God will reward you if you conduct yourself properly most of the time. That is, there is supposed to be a weighing of good versus evil deeds at the time of judgment. It is strange that they do not consider the fact that after death of the flesh, you would spend eternity as a spirit being. As a spirit being, it would be important to have a "right," or acceptable, spirit. Having the right spirit will not be some mystical event where your present spirit is changed after

---

6 If free will were not paramount, God would have created androids or animals that did not make choices but followed instinct and/or trained patterns of behavior. Without free will, there can be no faith. There are religious systems, today, as well as centuries ago, that deny the right to exercise free will and they will kill those who reject their concept of God. These religious systems are based upon the concept of rules and regulations, supposedly in order to please God. They have the mistaken belief that God is merely interested in and rewards us for the amount of control we exert over our own flesh's desires. This is nothing more than a form of brain washing. Why would God be interested in that as an objective for humanity? Our entire life would be considered a series of tests. Christians understand that God loves us, and His love is not dependent on our ability to successfully pass more tests than we fail. Jesus, His only begotten Son, died for us so that we could have the opportunity to be reconciled to Him through faith in Jesus.

7 Thus, the Father and the Holy Spirit are part of and expressed in Jesus. They are also one. More than merely having a common purpose, they are one in every way imaginable.

8 God neither compels nor drives people. In general, if you believe you are being driven or feel compelled, in any aspect of your life, and you cannot stop, it is more than likely an evil spirit is controlling that part of your life.

death. That process has to occur while you are still alive. Christianity is the only religion concerned with changing a person from the inside, from the spirit or heart, instead of trying to control a person's outward actions by imagined rewards for "acceptable" conduct.[9]

---

9 For example, Judaism, Islam, Hinduism, and Buddhism all use laws or rules to control the flesh and/or attempt to externally change the spirit by conduct or rituals. Often, their legal system is also based upon their religious laws. Most Christian countries, at least, have separate laws and a separate legal system for the lawless because they recognize that using a legal system for control purposes may make the society seem peaceable, but the citizens will have no freedom of choice concerning their "God."

GOD

IN THE BEGINNING—THE TRINITY[10]

GOD DOES EXIST![11] However, only Jesus can truly explain God. Therefore, it is very important to read what Jesus said, for He never lied and He was without sin. If He did lie, then He was not the ultimate and final sacrifice for man's sin. So what did Jesus say?

> All things are delivered unto me of my Father: and no man knoweth the Son, but the Father; neither knoweth any man the Father, save the Son, and he to whomsoever the Son will reveal him.
>
> —MATTHEW 11:27, KJV

> But if I do, though ye believe not me, believe the works: that ye may know, and believe, that the Father is in me, and I in him.
>
> —JOHN 10:38, KJV

> Why then do you accuse me of blasphemy because I said, "I am God's Son"? Do not believe me unless I do what my Father does. But if I do it, even though you do not believe me, believe the miracles, that you may know and understand that the Father is in me, and I in the Father."
>
> —JOHN 10:36–38

---

10 The term *Trinity* is a fourth-century word to explain how God has revealed Himself to man. He is composed of three parts: the Father, the Son, and the Holy Spirit. Basic Christianity states that God, or the Godhead, is composed of three equal, eternal, non-created essences or substances, known as the Father, the Son, and the Holy Spirit.

11 If you do not believe that God exists, it takes quite an imagination to contemplate the existence of anything including yourself. However, you know you exist because you are able to think. By extension, God must exist.

7

So Jesus said, "When you have lifted up the Son of man, then you will know that I am [the one I claim to be] and that I do nothing on my own but speak just what the Father has taught me. The one who sent me is with me; he has not left me alone, for I always do what pleases him."

—JOHN 8:28–29

And now, Father, glorify me in your presence with the glory I had with you before the world began.

—JOHN 17:5

Father, just as you are in me and I am in you. May they also be in us so that the world may believe that you have sent me. I have given them the glory that you gave me, that they may be one as we are one: I in them and you in me.

—JOHN 17:21–23

Jesus' statements do not support the conclusion that some have made that Jesus was an adopted Son of God who became that because of His virtuous, sinless life and sacrifice. He pre-existed man and was sent by the Father.[12] He also references the Holy Spirit as existing with the Father.

But the Comforter, (even) the Holy Spirit, whom the Father will send in my name, he shall teach you all things, and bring to your remembrance all that I said unto you.

—JOHN 14:26

---

12 While his human nature was formed within His mother's womb, His spirit, in His case but not man's, already existed. The reason for the Holy Spirit being involved in the creation of Jesus was simply the fact that Jesus had to be born without any sin being past down from an earthly father. God said the sins of the fathers would be passed down to the sons. Thus, for Jesus, to not to have had any sin, it was necessary that there be no earthly father involved. It also appears that Jesus had half-brothers (James, Joseph, Simon, and Judas) and a half-sister (Salome). Others may have also existed, but are not named. Joseph was probably much older than Mary and had a previous family. Did Mary remain a virgin? Matthew says Joseph did not "know her" until Jesus was born (Matt. 1:25) Thus, he did afterwards. Some writers also say Jesus was the firstborn, implying other children from Mary. However, this is not conclusive. Jesus committed the care of Mary to the apostle John while on the cross. History says Mary lived approximately fifteen more years. If she had other children under her care, there is no mention one way or the other. Joseph's children by a previous wife would have already been in their thirties or forties. Then again, some may have been Mary's also, and they were out on their own. The Bible does not mention Joseph being alive after Jesus is twelve years old. The evidence is not clear, but for James to accept the responsibility as the elder or bishop of the church in Jerusalem, he would have probably been older than Jesus; thus he would have had to be a half-brother.

The Bible indicates to us that the Holy Spirit was with the Father and He was sent by the Father to bestow blessings and gifts upon individuals such as John the Baptist (Luke 1:15, 41, 67; 2:25).[13] It is important also to note that the Holy Spirit has a different standing than Jesus because one can speak against the Father and Jesus, but whoever speaks against the Holy Spirit will not be forgiven (Matt. 12:32; Mark 3:29). Later, after Jesus' crucifixion, the Holy Spirit was sent to believers (Luke 11:13). However, there are different levels of inter-action. It can vary from the Spirit being within us to being filled by the Holy Spirit[14] to being baptized with the Holy Spirit.[15] These represent several levels of our relationship with the Holy Spirit.

As you can see, the concept of a triune God is clearly expressed and explained by Jesus in the Bible.[16] John and Paul write about the underlying facts, however the word *trinity* is not used. This concept, however, is probably one of the most important in Christianity.[17]

Some religions accept the concept of a single, almighty God. However, they cannot conceive of God being anything except singular in concept. They can accept that man can have at least a flesh and soul component (Jews equate the soul with the spirit), but when man was made in God's imagine, they picture God as looking like a human, rather than thinking that perhaps "in our image, in our likeness" (Gen. 1:26)[18] means "composed of more than one

---

13 Jesus, after His water baptism, was full of the Holy Spirit (Luke 4:1). Luke's statement does not mean He was not full of the Father and the Holy Spirit before then.

14 There are many infillings, as the needs and calling of the Holy Spirit arise, but there is only one baptism with the Holy Spirit.

15 Some would dispute this concept. Can people have a different anointing? If so, then just as with different anointing and gifts, it is feasible that there are different levels of interaction between our spirit and the Holy Spirit as our spiritual maturity develops and we grow in our relationship with Christ.

16 One concept that some "Christian" cults have is that Jesus was created by God, given a mission, and sent by the Father. Two questions are raised by this belief. First, can anything created ever really know the Father as Jesus claimed He did? Second, isn't it an insult to God to say that His love only extends to the point of creating some other being to be an atonement for man's sin if man believes that the created (Jesus) was the "Son" of God? How would God, in that scenario, compare with the standard that there is no greater love than to die for someone, in this case, His creation? (See John 15:13.) This created substitute concept appears to be a deception, which God is not capable of performing. That is something Satan, the father of all lies, would do.

17 It is an obstacle for the Jewish and Muslim religions, as well as some "Christian" cults.

18 Apparently, Moses did not have any problem with the use of the term *us* in Genesis and the term *God* in the First Commandment (Exod. 20:2)

part." Christianity is different because it teaches that we have three parts: flesh, soul, and spirit. Our soul is thought of as our intellect and memories as well as our mind, will, and emotions. Our spirit is thought of as that part that brings life to our flesh, that part of us that molds, influences, and shapes our thoughts and actions.

All "Christian" cults have a root belief that rejects a pre-Creation triune God. Mainly, they cannot accept the concept that Jesus preexisted the creation as part of God. Instead, they believe He was adopted by God as His Son while on Earth, or that He was created by God at the same time the angels were created but was superior to the angels. These concepts result from the pride of man being influenced by Satan. In other words, man believes he can determine who and what God is rather than trusting Jesus.

When we read the Old Testament, we see that the early writers generally did not refer to God as more than singular in nature. Hundreds of years later, the term *Holy Spirit* was used.[19] (See Isaiah 63:10, YLT, NKJV, KJV.) However, the connotation was of something imparted to us or as an active force at work within us.[20]

There are religions, not necessarily cults, that reject the concept of a Son of God existing before Creation, as well as existing before any indwelling in flesh. Some get around the concept of the Christian Trinity by claiming that all spirits at some point in time occupy human flesh and that they preexist human conception and return to God after death.

Jesus said He existed before Abraham was born (John 8:58). Jesus also said He came from God and was sent by God (John 8:42). Further, He was not of this world (John 8:23). Jesus proved His power and authority over all physical and spiritual realms while on Earth. However, if you do not believe Jesus was telling the truth about Himself, then you will not have the ability to believe in Him. On the other hand, if you can believe that He was telling the truth, then to be "sent" must mean that He preexisted His incarnation. Consequently, the Son of God did not become the Son after taking on human flesh.

The next question is whether the Son was created by God as a lesser creature than God but still superior to an angel. Or was He already a part of God? In other words, was Jesus in His preincarnate form merely a created, sacrificial

---

19 Apparently the separateness of the Holy Spirit was not recognized.

20 See also 1 Peter 1:12; Matthew 1:18; Matthew 28:19; Luke 2:25; and John 14:26.

Lamb for man's sin, while also God's Son?[21] The answer is given by John and Paul. Before God created time He separated Himself into three persons of equal stature but with different duties and/or purposes.[22] For some people this is a complex concept because they tend to think, as mentioned above, in terms of singularity and hierarchy or ranking. What makes this a matter of faith is that Jesus did not come right out and say, "We, the Father, the Son, and the Holy Spirit, are God." It is difficult to know whether the disciples would have understood this until after Jesus' resurrection. Therefore, He indirectly spoke about the Trinity. Perhaps the clearest indication is in John 17:21–23: "Father, just as you are in me and I am in you. May they also be in us so that the world may believe that you have sent me. I have given them the glory that you gave me, that they may be one as we are one: I in them and you in me."

Even the Old Testament indicated a plurality when God spoke of Himself. For example: "Then God said, 'Let us make man in our image, in our likeness'" (Gen. 1:26); "Come, let us go down" (Gen. 11:7); "Who will go for us?" (Isa. 6:8). Thus, the foundation for the doctrine of the Trinity was established before Jesus was born to Mary. However, the references Jesus made about Himself, the Father, and the Holy Spirit are the revelation presented about the nature of God. If one cannot accept Jesus as anything other than a good human, then he or she would be mistaken to believe His statements about God. However, once you can accept Jesus as existing before being incarnated and trust the representations He made about Himself, then the importance of who He really is—the Son of God—becomes clear. He was never just a good or even a sinless human being who was adopted by the Father as His Son.[23]

It is obvious that God recognizes man's mental limitations. He has chosen to reveal Himself as the Father, the Son, and the Holy Spirit. Yet, there is still

---

21 One way to help clarify the problem is to recognize that Jesus has a divine nature and a human nature, for a short time. When the Bible speaks of Jesus, you must be aware of which nature is being addressed. In heaven, it would clearly be His divine. While on Earth, it could be either. Clearly, He suffered in His human nature. However, most of the statements made by Jesus were from His divine nature, particularly relating to Himself, His miracles, the kingdom of God, and future events.

22 John said that the Father set apart Jesus as His very own and sent Him into the world (John 10:36). The New King James states that the Father sanctified and sent Him. (See also John 16:28 (NKJV), "I came forth from the Father;" and John 17:5) Today, we would use different wording, for example, "spun off," "divested," or "separated." However, none of these imply a separate creation of something that did not already exist. At the end, after Jesus destroys all His enemies and hands over the kingdom to the Father, then God will be all in all (1 Cor. 15:24–28).

23 Jewish legend would call an angel a "son" of God.

only one God,[24] not, as some would conclude, three gods working together in a cooperative effort for a common purpose.[25]

In John 1, John says that the Word was with God as well as *being* God. If you can accept the use of the term *Word* in this context as meaning the human who is called Jesus, it is clear that Jesus preexisted all things. In fact, through Him all things were created, including time itself (John 1:10).

In John 10:36, Jesus said that He was set apart by the Father and sent into the world. Jesus used the term *Son* to describe Himself.[26] Clearly, then, to be set apart He had to preexist in some form. You cannot assume that being set apart means a segregation and dedication of something that has its own separate agenda. Jesus carried out the plan of God that existed before anything was created by Him.[27]

As indicated above, the Bible tells us that before time Jesus was called *Logos* or *the Word* (John 1:1–2). The Son was sent, and we know Him now as Jesus (1 John 4:9).[28] Jesus demonstrated that He had many powers and He was not merely human. Yet, He could also understand how man could be tempted toward

---

24 It is strange that man sets himself up to determine the breadth and complexity of God. In addition, the rejection of the concept that God could be three and also one causes some religions to reject Jesus as the preincarnate Son (part) of God. Rather than rejecting the concept, perhaps before a position is taken rejecting it, one should require proof it cannot be true. With God, how can anyone define oneness? Surely, oneness is not defined by human standards.

25 Understand that there is a connection between the Father, Son, and Holy Spirit that cannot be understood by the human experience. They can exist as separated, yet still be connected enough that they are also one. For example, Jesus said He was in the Father and the Father was in Him (John 10:38).

26 In the flesh, we give birth as a means of multiplying. God does not take this approach. He can spin off or separate Himself. Afterwards, He is still one by those criteria God decided would be used to define oneness.

27 Clearly, when Jesus said He came from the Father and entered the world, He did not come into existence at the insemination of Mary, at the birth of Jesus, at the baptism of John, or at His death. He also did not become the Son because of His actions and lack of sin. If Jesus were purely a human creation, sin would have been passed down from the human father, and He could not have been a perfect, sinless sacrifice for man's sin. However, without an earthly father but having a divine father, the Holy Spirit, Jesus started life without sin.

28 Notice that John says He, Jesus, was sent. John did not say that after taking on human flesh or being born He became the Son. To be sent, one must already exist. (See also John 3:34; Galatians 4:4.) Jesus is described by John as the only begotten son of God (John 1:18; 3:16–18). *Only begotten* does not relate to birth but instead to a status of uniqueness.

evil,[29] and thus He knew man's feelings and weaknesses.[30] He also suffered more than man did, in that after His life span of approximately thirty years, He felt the agony of the separation from the Father. This is something we, in human flesh, have never experienced.

It is important to recognize that Jesus knew before He created anything that He would take on human flesh, suffer somewhat with its limitations, and die as a blood sacrifice as the ultimate and complete atonement for man's sins (Eph. 3:9; John 1:3). There is no alternative way to reconcile ourselves to God. Before His sacrifice, there was the Law. Afterward, adherence to the Law no longer had the same importance.

With Jesus' sacrifice, man moved into a new era or age. A new covenant replaced the old covenant. The new covenant is not merely an option. One must never conclude that the Law could ever be equal or superior to Jesus' sacrifice, for that is what it would be if His sacrifice were merely an alternative. It would also mean that God valued adherence to law more than faith in Him. That in turn would mean Satan could argue that the Law was more important than faith. And since he was not given any laws to follow before his rebellion, he and the other angels could argue that they could not have sinned. Moreover, for God to say otherwise would portray God as unjust in His judgment.[31]

Contrary to one school of thought, Jesus' sacrifice was actually foretold during Israel's early history. Of course, Jews are still waiting for the Messiah to appear. However, they had a very limited concept of what the purposes of the Messiah were two thousand years ago. For example, they thought He was

---

29 After Jesus was baptized by John the Baptist, Satan tried to tempt Jesus. Thus, Jesus experienced what temptation was all about in His human nature, but it was not a situation where Jesus was actually even close to giving credence to Satan's temptations for more than a few seconds of evaluation. Jesus knew who He was. Anyway, what were Satan's temptations? Two were for Jesus to prove who He was and the third was an attempt to bribe Jesus with something that was not important. (Why would Jesus even want the kingdoms of this world when He shared in the glory of the Father and knew by His divine nature how everything would end?) After forty days of fasting, Jesus' body may have been in a weak state, but His divine nature was even stronger from the time spent with the Father.

30 Perhaps the most important of these is our separation from God. This is what many believe Jesus felt when dying on the cross. In other words, Jesus felt the feeling of being separated from the Father, but to a much greater extent than we could feel since we have never had that bond.

31 This idea of the Law being paramount comes into play with the concept of dispensationalism, discussed later on in Chapter 9, which takes the position that Jesus' sacrifice is merely applicable for a period of time, or an intermission in the history of man, for the benefit of the Gentiles. With this belief, the adherence to the Law is the main reason for man's existence. This is contrary to Romans 3:27–29.

coming for the Jews only and not for all humanity. Some also thought He would appear as a fully grown man and become a military leader who would conquer their enemies.[32]

WHAT MUST YOU DO?

Acceptance of the Trinity is basic to Christianity. Jesus died as the way for all men to pass through His sacrifice into salvation. Nevertheless, we have a part to perform. It is an active part, not a passive part. We begin with a step of faith by accepting Him into our hearts (Rom. 10:9–10). To do this we have to invite His Spirit into ourselves. Mental acceptance is not enough. Paul states that the belief and faith must be within your heart. It must become part of your innermost being (Heb. 10:22).[33]

CITATIONS REFERENCING THE PRE-EXISTENCE OF JESUS

The one whom the Father set apart as his very own and sent into the world.

—JOHN 10:36

- Only Jesus has seen the Father and was present with Him: Luke 10:22; John 6:46; 8:38;[34] 17:5, 24
- Jesus was sent by the Father: John 7:28–29; 8:42; 10:36; 16:28; 17:18
- The Father and Jesus are one: John 8:29; 10:38; 14:10–11; 16:32; 17:11, 21

Other citations relating to time: 2 Timothy 1:9–10; John 1:1; 8:58

SUMMARY OF MAJOR POINTS

- God has revealed Himself to humanity as one God, consisting of the Father, Son, and Holy Spirit.

---

32 The Jews were focused on their own small world and considered themselves to be special to God and that the rest of humanity was, in comparison, unimportant to Him.

33 It is unproven that Paul was the author of Hebrews. It could have been Barnabas. However, the majority of scholars believe it was Paul.

34 In Exodus 3:14, when asked by Moses for His name, God said to tell the Israelites that "I AM" sent him. In John 8:58, Jesus said, "Before Abraham was born, I am!"

- The Son, Jesus, was set apart. He also created all things (for example, time, the universe, angels, humanity).
- Jesus knew before Creation that He would become the atonement for man's sin. At the end, God will be our all in all (1 Cor. 15:24–28).[35]

---

35 Perhaps all, including time, will be merged together with God. If so, it could explain why God could not merge with evil and only the righteous could dwell with God.

?
2

ANGELS AND THE UNIVERSE

FIRST, GOD CREATED TIME

IME IS THE result of change. In other words, changes in position of a subatomic particle or energy wave occur over time, such that minute relocations in position must use or create time. Even the creation of energy waves, or whatever was the first thing to change, caused time to come into existence. God, however, is not subject to time and thus does not change. He can both exist outside of time as well as interact with all that is subject to time, without changing.

Being above and beyond time, God is not affected by it, yet He sees into the future. This has caused some confusion over the years because many have thought that this means there is one path for the history of time, including the universe, both visible and the invisible, as well as for angels and humanity. That view, however, discounts the exercise of free will by angels and man. God, however, is unlimited in His ability to predict all events relating to nature, as well as all acts, decisions, and choices made by all created beings since before anything, including time, was created.[36] In essence, He does know the future, because He knew all possible outcomes of events before they even had the opportunity of occurring. Consequently, angels and man can exercise their free will, and the future is not predetermined along a single path. Instead, there are multiple paths. In other words, it is clearly within God's capability to have determined before time began all possible choices; events; or happenings of humanity, Satan, or nature before Creation actually started. With that information, God could develop a plan for all creation that allows for the exercise of free will and set it in motion, yet also have the conclusion He wants.

The act of trusting in that conclusion contains within it the development of and reliance upon faith in Him. Why is this important to understand? Because

---

36 With God, there is no infinity. Everything is known. Even time itself exists because God wills it. Once it has served its purpose, it will cease to exist.

before He created anything, Jesus[37] knew about the rebellion of the angels, the fall of man, Abraham, Israel's failures, the need for His incarnation, His death, His resurrection, His second coming, and the establishment of the kingdom of God.[38]

For those who reject a Creator, there are three possibilities used to explain how the angels, the earth, and humans came into existence. First, God just stumbled upon the earth while it was in an evolutionary phase and He tinkered with it and created animals, plants, and man. Second, He did not do anything at all, but just adopted it. Third, He created everything, including, in the process, time.[39] In the first and second cases, He just watched until the right time to intercede.[40] In order to support the first two cases, you must believe that God is incapable of creating the earth or both the earth and all life, not to mention the angels.[41] If you doubt God is the Creator of the entire universe, both the visible and the invisible, then perhaps if you understand the reason for man's existence, the rest will be understood.

---

37 Genesis says God created the universe, but Ephesians 3:9 and Colossians 1:15–16 are more specific in that it states Creation occurred through Jesus. The Old Testament writers' revelation concerning God appears to be limited to a single identity because God did not clearly describe the other persons of the Trinity (though the word *us* was used in Genesis 3:22 and elsewhere).

38 Many so-called Christian denominations will acknowledge that God created humanity, but they have trouble accepting the fact Jesus had any part with the Creation. As pointed out earlier, Jesus is part of God and He preexisted all creation. In the end God will be all in all (1 Cor. 15:28).

39 Time began when something changed. It could have been a conversion of energy into matter. Matter then contained particles at the atomic level that moved position or fluctuated somehow. Change automatically creates time because there is a "before" and "after" aspect to existence. Thus, for any change to occur, it must occur over "time," no matter how small the moment is that lapses.

40 Recognize that for this scenario to occur somehow time already has to exist.

41 This is true only if you think that God was created, as well as the angels, by something else. However, if you continue that logic of trying to find the ultimate source of the first creator, you would have to continue out to infinity. That exercise is going to be unfruitful, and it will lead you to believe there is no God. Of course, it would be merely an exercise of your pride seeking answers that do not exist. There appears, according to Christian traditions, to be the following hierarchy, subdivided into three orders of angels: the first order of seraphim, cherubim, and ophanim; a second order of thrones, dominions, and principalities; and a third order of powers, archangels, and angels. The "ranking" of these angels is unclear. (There may be another identified as lordships.) However, Paul stated that dominion, authority, and power would be destroyed by Jesus (1 Cor. 15:24). This tends to indicate that some of them are under Satan's control. It is unclear in which order Lucifer existed (Ezek. 28:11–19). He is commonly considered an archangel, however, the New Testament only names Michael as belonging to this class. Gabriel is also considered an archangel, though he may have been a cherub.

Second, God Created Angels

While few have actually seen angels, many have encountered evil spirits, even if they did not know it at the time.[42] If they have not felt the effects personally, they have encountered them in others. If you do believe in God, you obviously believe there is a spiritual realm of existence. Given this, who but God could have created the angels? In fact, as stated earlier, God created everything, including the earth. However, He probably would have created it to look as if He did not actually create any of it, so that man would not be able to "prove" that God exists. In fact, what evidence man can develop tends to suggest, to some people, that God did not create the universe.

God desires faith.[43] This also includes love and trust from those who were created. In order to have faith generated within man's spirit, there must not be any overt or tangible evidence of God's existence. Thus, it was necessary to create the universe without any tangible or measureable evidence of His work. In fact, evidence of evolution would have been purposely created as an obstacle, thus creating the dilemma, does man believe his eyes and scientific evidence, or does he seek another answer? Once you know that God exists, the answer is obvious. He created the world to look like it evolved, because to do otherwise would be to prevent or hinder the growth of faith.

Is it any wonder then, that there has been no evidence that would conclusively prove that God created the earth? If you could imagine you were God for a moment and you wanted to give an opportunity for faith to come into existence, would you create anything that could be investigated and proven by man to have been created by God? In fact, if you were able to determine all of the possible outcomes of man's scientific and technological development and decisions he would make, why could you not also make creation such that it would be *impossible* for man to prove that the earth, animals, and humanity were created? You would make creation so that man, with his limited mental capacity, would conclude just the opposite. In other words, creation would have occurred in such a way that "clues" would lead away from the concept of a creator. Evidence would support the belief that man and animals evolved and

---

42 One-third of the angels rebelled against God, and they have been cast out of heaven to roam the earth until judgment, after which they will be set apart from God and the saints. For more information, see *Pigs in the Parlor* by Frank and Ida Mae Hammond (Impact Christian Books, 1990). It appears that children in Christ may have guardian angels interceding for them (Matt. 18:10).

43 Apparently, some of the angels did not have faith in God even though evidence was all around them. Thus, evidence of God does not mean that faith is guaranteed. However, man will prove that faith in God can exist without first having demonstrative evidence of God.

the universe was a cosmic accident. Thus, man's scientific evidence, even though many aspects of it are inconclusive, achieves its goal of indirectly strengthening the need for faith, particularly for those who do not know Jesus. Knowing Jesus causes the wisdom of God to show us how prideful man's limited knowledge is concerning creation.

To prove God's fairness and justice after the fall of some of the angels, the plan was that man would be created. Since then, man has gone through different relationship periods with God. Initially there were traditions concerning things that man ought to do that were passed down as part of man's oral history. Later, there were written or codified laws and finally a period of faith. Only in this last period, however, has there been a development of the spiritual relationship between man and God that develops the love and trust necessary to fulfill God's purpose of creation. However, this is only achieved through Jesus, as will be explained latter.

Naturally, God could not exclude Satan, the leader of the rebellious angels, from influencing man's history. It would not be fair, so Satan would argue. (Neither would it have achieved God's purposes of a faith-based existence.) Thus, Satan has a certain amount of influence, by God's permission, in the lives of humanity. This again demonstrates the fairness of God. The fallen angels—demons—can tempt, influence, and in certain limited cases control man. Examples of their influence are reflected in the Gospels.

Where is Satan now? There is nothing in the letters of Paul that indicates that Satan has already incurred his final judgment and that he is no longer at war with us. Thus, one should expect demons to be operating just as they did two thousand years ago. The difference now, however, is that man has access to weapons through Jesus to overcome and defeat him. It is a battle, however, for which the church does a poor job preparing Christians. Either they ignore the need, make little mention of the situation, or they go to religious extremes.

Demons can cause sickness as well as merely influence the mind, such as in causing temptations to sin. They can also partially or fully inhabit man and affect their emotions, thoughts, and desires. Generally, however, they have to be given permission in order to be able to enter us.[44] This is usually not an overt voluntary act on our part but is a result of some tacit approval or allowance

---

44 Fortunately, for Christians, demons cannot possess us. They can influence us from without and within. Part of the sanctification process, to be explained in more detail later on, may involve the cleansing or purification of our spirit. However, this cannot be achieved using external means, but only by the working of the Holy Spirit in conjunction with our will and spirit. Obeying laws or chastening our flesh, which will deceive those who can merely observe the outward acts of our flesh-man, will not purify our spirit. It amounts to hypocrisy, one of the situations Jesus often spoke against.

from us. Sometimes they are passed down from generation to generation in the form of generational patterns.

Regardless, you can be delivered. If spiritually mature enough, in other words, sometime after the baptism with the Holy Spirit, you can pray for your own deliverance through the power of the Holy Spirit.

ANGELS AND FREE WILL

Angels were and still are subject to the limitations of time. They had free will.[45] We also know that angels had an organization in which some had rank and/ or position with power and authority to carry out responsibilities.[46] Angels do not marry (Mark 12:25), and they do not die (Luke 20:35). We do not worship angels (Col 2:8); in fact, the saints will judge them.[47]

There appears to be seven archangels who have the highest levels of responsibility in their interaction with man.[48] Gabriel is the chief messenger. Michael is the warrior, at least later on after the rebellion. Raphael is a healing angel.[49] In addition, Lucifer, an angel of beauty, was in charge of praise. Lucifer apparently thought he was very important, so much so that he challenged God.[50] He,

---

45 Free will is very, very important to God. Otherwise, He would have created robots or pets. How could He have a relationship with anything that did not have the free will to make choices? Nevertheless, as with our own children, we are disappointed when they make the wrong choices. However, we would not want them to be limited in their choices, for any reason. Thus we, as God surely does, experience both joy and sadness because of our children's choices.

46 Some are known as "thrones," "dominions," "principalities," "powers," and "authorities." (See Colossians 1:16 and 1 Peter 3:22.)

47 Angels started in a state without sin and one-third moved into sin. Man starts in sin and seeks to move into a state without sin, which can only be accomplished with and through Jesus. We Christians, as saints, will probably be judging angels from our witness or from a representative standard, as opposed to the individual judgment of each fallen angel, by us.

48 Revelation 8:2 indicates seven archangels. Their names, except for that of Michael and Gabriel, are not used in the New Testament.

49 In the Book of Tobit 12:15, part of the Apocrypha, Raphael is mentioned as a healing archangel. It is unclear what he did before the fall of man.

50 If one cannot remember his existence before time began, how could he possibly challenge our Creator, who created time and everything that is subject to time? Perhaps Satan believed God was created also.

as well as one-third of the angels who believed and followed his influence, was banished from the presence of God[51] to Earth.[52]

Why is it important to know this sequence? It becomes important to our understanding of man's history of existence with God. It is also important that Jesus knew of the angels' rebellion and banishment before they were even created.[53] With that background, the next major event was man's creation and fall. God expected the Fall, and His response to it was anticipated before it occurred.[54]

The significance for us is that the fallen angels, at least some of them, interact with us. They exist outside of us and speak to our minds in an attempt to influence us. However, their most effective evil occurs when they are able to exist within us. Usually, unless inherited from our parents, they have to be invited, either directly or indirectly, to enter us.

Why did angels have free will? Being persuaded by any influence short of torture is generally regarded as an exercise of your free will. You can chose to ignore a need or desire, or you can satisfy or comply with it after weighing all factors. If it is a law and you weigh the consequences of not following it and decide it would be better to follow the law rather than not follow it, it is still an exercise of your free will. God wants your choice to follow or obey Him to be "free" and to come from your love and trust in Him, not from a reward-and-punishment existence.

God knows that with competing influences around us and with our many

---

51 The angels' rebellion, particularly their pride, was sinful. Sin and the taint of sin upon the spirit will keep one from spending eternity in the presence of God. Satan may have limited access to God for the time being based upon statements in the Book of Job.

52 We know that Eve was spoken to by Satan in the form of a serpent. Whether Satan was cast down to the earth before humanity was created or afterward is unknown. It appears to be more likely that the garden was created after the angels were cast down to a place without much of what we now know as Earth. In other words, the present earth, with its land, seas, and animals, was created as a prelude to the creation of man, but perhaps after the casting down of the angels.

53 The mere fact that some of the angels did rebel indicates that angels could exercise their free will in making choices. Thus, they were not under any compulsion, nor were they "programmed" with responses and decision-making parameters that could not be violated. In other words, they were not robots limited to their programming. Man was also created with free will, which is a very important factor that affects our relationship with God. Without free will, there can be no faith.

54 The fact that it was expected by God does not mean that God is the source of evil or sin. It merely means that with free will, as with angels and humanity, being imperfect, bad decisions will be made, eventually. However, it is not the wrong decisions that are the problem; it is the reason for those decisions. If they were caused by pride, resentment, hate, bitterness, greed, envy, etc., all the opposite of love, then our spirit is incompatible with God's and there can be no coexistence.

limitations, our choices will often turn out to be wrong or at least not the most desirable choices. Fortunately, however, there have been times in man's history in which he has been righteous even though he was not sinless. Therefore, our wrong or imperfect choices did not keep us from being righteous.[55] However, the wrong spirit would keep man from being righteous. For centuries, the central issue had been man's ability to adhere to the Law. However, Jesus changed that and implemented His plan that made the central issue one of faith in Him. The Law served to change a man's behavior, not change a man's spirit. Faith, on the other hand—that is, faith in Jesus—changes our spirit.

ANGELS—LAW VS. FAITH

Angels, as stated earlier, exercised free will rather than acting under any compulsion from God when they made a decision or choice on whether to join or follow Lucifer in his rebellion against God. It is likely that the angels did not have any published rules to follow.[56] If they had, and they went against them, there might not have been any reason to create man. In other words, if there had been known rules against rebellion, then the need to create man to show that faith was better than laws does not really make much sense. However, if there were no established rules, then the proof that the followers of Lucifer should have had faith in God would need to be demonstrated to prove God's justice. This demonstration was the reason for man's creation. A creature that did not have the advantage of an existence in the presence of God yet by faith could know within himself that God was good and could be trusted above all else.

To help clarify what is meant above, imagine this scenario: Lucifer, by whatever means, influences a significant minority of angels to follow his leadership instead of God's. When the consequences are the removal of his followers from heaven, Satan challenges God, arguing that God is unfair because there were no rules prohibiting what Satan did.[57] God, to prove His fairness and justice,

---

55 *Righteous* in this context means having a right relationship with God.

56 Man, regardless of the label he uses to describe his belief in God, often wants to resort to obeying rules. In addition, because he knows he will not be perfect, he wants God to balance his "good" actions against his "evil" actions. That is the underlying principle of Judaism, Islam, and other faiths. Naturally, following God's will is the most important purpose of life. God, however, is not seeking obedience but rather a different heart or spirit than man generally has. Many Jewish scholars, in rejecting Jesus, cannot understand that God desires actions born of a pure spirit that arises because of love, faith, and trust in Him. God is not merely looking for decisions and actions that are not sinful.

57 Apparently, Satan lifted himself up against God. (Isaiah 14:12; 45:7)

decided to demonstrate that faith in Him was what was required, as illustrated by the majority of angels who did not follow Satan. In addition, that faith could manifest itself, even in creatures that did not have the advantage of knowing God. Consequently, man was created.

Satan, however, was not content, and he wanted permission to attack God's new creation. Satan was given limited permission and power. Remember, however, that God, even before He created anything, knew the likelihood of all of these events taking place. Also remember that the exercise of free will automatically means that some choices are going to be self-serving, so long as any creature recognizes it has authority to make decisions that fulfill its own desires. This becomes a problem when one's own self becomes first in priority. In other words, if your love of God is less than the love of your self, God's desires are subordinated to your own desires. However, if by faith one loves God first, then one's own desires will be less important.

So where does Jesus fit into this scenario? Because man sinned, even to the point of shedding the blood that maintains a body's life, something had to occur to offset the sin and to bring man's spirit to a sinless state. The highest possible sacrifice for sin was that God Himself would allow His creation to shed His blood while incarnating Himself with human nature. Thus, Jesus, a part of God, who actually created all that was created, took on human flesh by being born through woman.[58] He lived and spread the message that belief and faith in Him would allow our sin to be removed. Only then would we be able to be in His presence for the remainder of existence.

To summarize, imagine a confrontation between God and Satan where Satan, like in the Book of Job,[59] challenges God by claiming that He was unfair to condemn him and his followers for their rebellion because there were no laws or rules that told them what they could and could not do. However, God knew that it was not about obedience to laws. God was not after perfect obedience

---

58 Early Jewish traditions expected a Messiah to come and establish the kingdom of God on Earth. They expected the Messiah to take the form of a man. However, it was generally thought that he would just appear as a mature man, already grown. The concept of a Messiah being born human and growing up experiencing life was not imaginable. Naturally, the concept that part of God could take on human form was also not imaginable. To the Jew, the Messiah was expected to be a prophet who had attained that status through discipline and knowledge, after which God would place on him the authority of a prophet. (In essence, he would be a super-prophet, above all other previous prophets.) Another view was that he would be a warrior that would conquer the current oppressors. Few expected the Messiah to be like Jesus. To the Jew, God is singular in existence and God cannot be anything else. Jews still believe in this limited concept of the Godhead.

59 This book appears to have been written after the Flood but before the Exodus of the Jews from Egypt.

to rules. Instead, what He wanted was faith and trust in Him[60] at a level that reflected the angels' complete love and trust in God. Thus, the angels' choice to follow God should have been based upon the nature, or purity, of their heart.[61] With complete freedom of choice, their choice always should have been to place faith and trust in God first. To prove to Satan and all creation the justification for the concept of faith rather than obedience to laws, man was created. This was also planned for before the beginning of time.[62] Satan and his followers, the angels cast out from heaven (aka demons), were not immediately cast into hell because of their lack of faith and trust in God. Instead, they have been given an opportunity to demonstrate that God is unjust in His judgment of them.

FALLEN ANGELS—THEIR INFLUENCE[63]

The angels were subjected to the temptations and persuasion of Lucifer before their fall, perhaps promises of some better situation under his authority.[64] We

---

60 In our world, blind faith is not warranted and can be dangerous. In God's world, you can put your complete trust and faith in God.

61 Did God create evil? It is recorded in Isaiah 45:7 (KJV) that God created evil. However, perhaps a more accurate statement would be that when God created creatures with free will to make choices, the potential for evil was created. (The verbiage of other versions, such as the NKJV and NIV does not indicate that God created evil.) A byproduct of the right to make choices creates the potential that we will place our own desires first. In that indirect way, God created the potential for evil, but He did not create it as if good and evil are substances like trees, water, sunlight, atoms, and energy. Our choices, however, will often be motivated by the level of purity of our heart or spirit.

62 Remember, however, that God knew this would occur before He created anything. He also knew that wrong motives would cause wrong choices, which could be sinful. He also knew they would have to be purged, and only His own sacrifice would be adequate.

63 Evil spirits are real. God forbade contacting them to discover the future. Witchcraft, voodoo, magic, excluding sleight of hand tricks, mysticism, and other satanic practices open the door for demons to enter us. The term *ghost*, although generally used in the Old Testament to mean "spirit," is acknowledged even in the New Testament. For example, when Jesus was walking on the lake after the boat left the shore, the disciples thought they saw a ghost. (See Matthew 14:26.) After His resurrection, He appeared and the two travelers thought He was a ghost. Note that Jesus did not say they did not exist; instead, He pointed out that He had flesh and bones, and that ghosts do not have a physical body. (See Luke 24:39.)

64 Imagine what it was like in heaven before the fall of Lucifer. The angels likely didn't know what evil was. They were in an existence where God's goodness was everywhere. Some of the angels, however, moved from that state into a state of sin by listening to, trusting, and then exercising their free will, for the wrong reasons, and aligning themselves with Lucifer. The consequence of their choice was probably unknown. We, on the other hand, are well familiar with sin and want to move into a state free of sin. The fallen angels and Satan do not want us to achieve that goal.

do not really have any indication of the arguments and lies Lucifer used to cause one-third of the angels to align themselves with him. It was necessary that if humanity were to be the instrument used to prove God's justice and fairness, man must also be subjected to temptations, lies, and deception.

Satan became the personification of all that was evil, that is, all that denies and rejects complete faith in God. Satan uses any means available, within the limitations placed by God. Thus, some of the fallen angels assist in Satan's plans to convince people that God is unfair and unjust.[65] This ability is given by permission from God so Satan will not have any excuses when he is proven wrong. These fallen angels have a structure or ruling order. Some are from the ranks known as powers, authorities, and principalities. (See Ephesians 3:10; 6:12; Colossians 1:16; 2:15; 1 Peter 3:22. The wording in the King James Version is clearest.) The higher the rank within the order the more influence and power the demon has from Satan.

The first temptation of man is recorded as that in the Garden of Eden. Of the two human beings created, Satan went to the one who did not have as long of a relationship with God and the one who had not directly heard what God said about the tree of the knowledge of good and evil.[66] In fact, the woman, Eve, was created after God told Adam to avoid eating fruit from the tree. Satan, who recognized that beings that get information secondhand do not always have 100 percent confidence in what is stated, asked Eve a basic question to test the understanding of Eve concerning the fruit in the Garden. Eve recited her understanding she had received from Adam. However, it was in error because God did not say they could not touch the fruit (Gen. 3:3). Thus, Satan immediately knew that Eve was not clear on the prohibition and attributed selfish motives to God for His prohibition against eating the fruit. Satan said they would not die, but instead, would become like God knowing good from evil. Satan created doubt in her mind about Adam's credibility or accuracy in relaying the instructions about the fruit. However, more than that, he played upon man's desire for a more intimate relationship with God and implied that

---

65 There is no higher or more pure being than God. Thus, if He is going to prove that He is just, He would have to prove it to Himself. His own integrity causes Him to allow Satan some leeway in his war with humanity. However, as a Christian we must learn how to defeat Satan by and through Jesus.

66 See Genesis 2:17. Understand that Adam probably did not even know what the words good and evil even meant. Perhaps Adam and Eve did not even know what "die" even meant.

this would occur if man became more like God (Gen. 3:5, KJV).[67] The Bible does not explain how Eve came to believe that knowing good and evil would cause man to gain wisdom (Gen. 3:6). It is clear, however, that it appears that one of Satan's primary functions is to tempt humanity.[68] In furtherance of that, he has the angels cast out of heaven to help him.

Soon after Adam's fall, man's rebellion and pride began to surface. It is first recorded in Cain's sacrifice to God. After Cain made a sacrifice to God that was not acceptable, Cain was troubled. God warned him that sin stood at the door (probably a reference to his heart), that sin sought to have him, and that Cain needed to master it (Gen. 4:6-7). What was God talking about? It appears that Cain was experiencing several emotions. Probably the strongest was rejection. Rejection, or rather the desire to overcome it, can be a powerful reason to sin. If a spirit of rejection comes into a person, then everything he does is influenced, to one degree or another, by trying to overcome those feelings. Accompanying a spirit of rejection, one that may have an even more profound impact, is a religious spirit. A religious spirit is always trying to justify itself to God by its religious activity and actions.[69] Thus, it causes a person to become extremely religious in whatever religious belief system they have chosen. It not only occurs in Islam, but in all religions, Judaism, Hinduism, Buddhism, and Christianity.

It is unfortunate that even Christians can fall under a religious spirit's influence. It is subtle, but it deludes a person into believing they have a special relationship with God.[70] The underlying mission of a religious spirit is to make a person continually attempt to justify themselves to God. In milder cases, it can make a person create or seek out a set of codes or laws that they can follow. The worse case often manifests itself by creating the belief or the need

---

67 It is interesting that in the King James Version of Genesis 3:5, Satan said that Adam and Eve could become "as gods." Most other Bibles, including the New King James Version, use the phrase "like God." Perhaps the temptation to Eve was similar to that which Satan made to the other angels. Satan had no concern about how his lies and evil would ultimately affect the angels that trusted him because of his position. In a similar manner, man often trusts a person because of that person's position.

68 Lucifer was in charge of praise, an angel of beauty. He wants to show the weakness of man and that God is wrong and unjust.

69 Jesus quite often was challenging the Jewish leaders who had proud spirits, in other words, those who outwardly displayed their "righteousness" for all others to see so they would be thought to be righteous. Those with religious spirits will often seek positions of influence in order to be lifted up by others.

70 Deceived people are sometimes the most religious.

in a person that they must become the "protector" of their faith. (Think of the actions of the church during the Dark Ages, the Crusades, the Inquisition, or extreme religious Muslims today.) They have no problem with killing other people when they believe they are doing so for God.[71]

A third spirit that is important to Satan is the spirit of Antichrist. Satan, of course, is the ultimate spirit warring God. However, he has another whose function is to create any thing that could minimize Jesus' impact on the world. Although Satan cannot see into the future as God can, he does have enough intelligence and historical information to guess which strategies might adversely affect God's plans. Thus, both before and after Jesus came, ideas and concepts have sprouted up that appear to diminish Jesus.

For example, 1,900 years ago, there were the Gnostics and Ebonites.[72] They attacked the divinity of Jesus by spreading the concept that Jesus was merely a good man whom God adopted as His Son. Even today, there are organizations who desire to call themselves Christian but deny the Trinity.[73] Naturally, there are other religions in the world that are very clear in their denial of the Trinity, such as Islam and Judaism. (They have a problem with the definition of one God, that is, limiting God to only their understanding of oneness.)

Today, we sometimes think of the Antichrist as an evil person with special, supernatural, satanic powers.[74] Thus, we have focused on the fleshly manifestation rather than the spiritual manifestation. This has become a diversion. In a similar manner, some in the church have misinterpreted the great whore or the harlot church in Revelation as the Catholic Church. The harlot church is a combined manifestation of the spirit of Antichrist in the guise of a Christian

---

71 Today, this would manifest itself in the form of terrorists and those who kill abortion doctors because of their beliefs.

72 Their purpose was to question and/or reject, sometimes overtly and sometimes subtlety, the preincarnate divinity of Jesus. They produced many of the apocryphal Gospels during the second century.

73 Simply put, their definition of Jesus denies who He was, in particular, that He preexisted man and took upon Himself the limitations of man in order to serve as a perfect sacrifice.

74 This is a popular belief not supported in the Book of Revelation. John mentions the Antichrist in 1 John and 2 John. Paul mentions "son of perdition" in 2 Thessalonians 2:1–12 (ASV, DNT, KJV, NKJV). Early Protestant reformers, including Martin Luther, thought of the Pope as the Antichrist. Some believe it will be a person resurrected by Satan who will have special powers. However, there is no clear biblical description of an actual person. John uses allegorical descriptions in Revelation, such as a beast with ten horns and seven heads.

church. No single organization comprises the harlot church.[75] A typical manifestation is any Christian group that denies the preincarnate Jesus or believes that God created Jesus.[76] Another example, however, would be those who accept the salvation brought through Jesus but deny the power and continual working of the Holy Spirit now.[77] This includes Christian groups that limit God's plan by denying its present applicability in the belief that the more general gifts to a church, such as prophecy, ministry, teaching, exhortation, giving, leading, and mercy; or the more individualized gifts of the word of wisdom, the word of knowledge, gift of faith, gifts of healings, the working of miracles, prophecy, discerning of spirits, tongues, and the interpretation of tongues from the Holy Spirit were only for the early period of the church's establishment.[78]

Did demons go away? No. They have even moved beyond mere temptation to actual interaction and interference with man. This was reflected in the beliefs expressed by the witnesses to Jesus' ministry. Possession, sickness, illness, and infirmities were often believed to have been caused by demons, usually as a result of some sin in the person's life or even their ancestor's life. In demonstrating the power of the kingdom of God, Jesus demonstrated His dominion over all spirits, all matter, all flesh, and even over the death of the human body.

How do demons influence us today?[79] Their influence is greatly diminished

---

75 At the time John was writing this book (circa A.D. 67 or 95), the Gnostics were pushing their beliefs denying Jesus' true self. If it was written in A.D. 95, Jerusalem had been destroyed and Christians were being persecuted. If it was A.D. 67, Jerusalem was under attack and Nero was killing Christians.

76 Thus, instead of the ultimate, perfect sacrifice for sin, Jesus is merely an anointed prophet that God adopts as His Son because of his martyrdom, or He was a sacrifice created by God and sent to the earth, but He was not part of the Godhead.

77 Some churches even deny that the Holy Spirit is also part of the Godhead. They believe He is merely a force from God.

78 They still believe in salvation through Jesus and only through Jesus. However, they have established themselves as the decision-makers on what God is still doing in the world. They have elevated their collective intellect, above all others, and they have created a church that is the Antichrist because they deny the present fullness of Christ and the Holy Spirit. Thus, to them the New Testament workings of the Holy Spirit stopped long ago. Again, this is an example of the manifestation in people with religious spirits. They rationalize that any lack of the evidence of the baptism with the Holy Spirit within them is because God changed the plan rather than really addressing the issue that perhaps there is something wrong with their spirit.

79 The following are recommended if more information is needed. *Deliverance from Evil Spirits* by Francis MacNutt (Chosen Books, 1995); and *The Handbook for Spiritual Warfare*, by Dr. Ed Murphy (Thomas Nelson, 2003).

when Christians are involved. Nevertheless, demons have two main areas of attack: one is our emotions, which affect our actions; and the other is our body, including both mental and physical qualities. Concerning physical infirmities, fortunately, humanity has been able to develop medicines and other treatments that counteract many demonic manifestations in our body.[80] Often, medical science, with both direct and indirect assistance by God, is able to discover a cause-and-effect relationship and then develop a chemical compound, or find it already existing in nature, to overcome the symptoms. What they have not always been able to discover is the actual cause of the problem. One reason is that it is possible that demons can affect a person's brain[81] or genes, as well as cause a malfunctioning of our organs. In so doing, they are often able to hide any obvious effect of their influence and power.

In early biblical times, there was an over simplification when blaming demons for problems that could have been caused by various other reasons, such as malnutrition. It is clear that our body will fail if we live long enough. Environmental factors can adversely affect our body. Therefore, Satan and his demons cannot be assigned the blame for all illness or diseases. For some things, however, Satan is the source, but he hides or camouflages himself. Why? So we will not use the weapons Jesus has given us. The most powerful of these weapons are a pure spirit and faith. With these, we are able to follow Paul's challenge in 2 Corinthians 10:4–6 (NKJV):

> For the weapons of our warfare are not carnal but mighty in God for pulling down strongholds, casting down arguments and every high thing that exalts itself against the knowledge of God, bringing every thought into captivity to the obedience of Christ, and being ready to punish all disobedience when your obedience is fulfilled.

Paul's challenge is not, however, a judgmental or combative attitude against man but rather against Satan. These battles are not for public display or to draw attention to ourselves.

A more difficult area concerns mental problems. Again, science has investigated behavior and has often labeled or categorized behavior patterns.

---

80 It is clear that Satan would not give inspiration to the medical scientists for development of cures.

81 For example, a spirit of addiction can affect a specific area of the brain that would cause the body and the brain to desire a particular substance. Addictions are not instantaneous but occur over time with the exposure to the substance. This is the typical means of a spirit entering a person. The repeated acts give tacit approval for their entry. Then once inside, they have to be expelled, for they will not leave on their own unless specially denied permission to remain.

Sometimes they have developed chemicals to hamper or prevent the outward manifestations of mental problems. The reason for the problem is not always clear. It may be physical in nature, such as a chemical imbalance. Then again, a demon could cause the same manifestation. There are, however, means to discover the difference. However, the physical reasons should be eliminated first, if possible. Unfortunately, few people are qualified to discern when a demon is involved. Generally, it would not be up to a medical professional to decide.

For the large majority of us, the manifestations are less severe. This is particularly true for Christians. There is a distinction between Satan's demonic manifestations in Africa and those in the West. In countries with more educated people, he attacks in subtle ways, such as through one's emotions and feelings of rejection, unworthiness, or fear.[82] For these and other emotions, he will cause a heightened dominance of that emotion through the work of an indwelling spirit. Be assured, however, that no evil spirit can take possession of a Christian because of the spirit of Jesus within us. Unfortunately, having Jesus within us does not rob Satan of an opportunity to continue to manipulate us if we already have any spirits. But fortunately, if they merely affect our emotions, we can change or overcome them by the leading of the Holy Spirit and through prayer. If more is involved than our emotions, such as controlling our personality traits, it will take additional effort and faith for deliverance. However, if still unsuccessful, spiritual counseling will be needed. Fortunately, as you go through the process, your spirit will conform with the Spirit of Jesus, which is part of the sanctification experience.

How do they enter us?

Here are some ways we give permission to demons:

- When you seek them out, such as by seeking information about your future or calling upon them to help accomplish a specific goal
- When there is a weak area in your life. Weak areas can include anger, feelings of rejection, or sinful acts. If one dwells upon

---

82 Satan also attacks by causing us to be prideful, to have jealousy, greed, envy, and so forth, to the extent that it affects our decisions and actions. Usually, for most people, these attacks are subtle. How do we recognize these as attacks of Satan? By becoming sensitive to the Holy Spirit, who will cause us to hesitate, question, or pause before we make a final commitment to sin. The baptism with the Holy Spirit and the sanctification process that occurs after salvation also make us more sensitive.

and/or allows it to dominate your life, you tacitly invite a spirit
to take over and control that area of your life.

- Playing around with spiritual games
- Worshiping nature instead of God
- Becoming cause-oriented, in other words, become too driven
  for a "good" cause
- Becoming religious in an effort to justify yourself to God

How do evil spirits within us manifest themselves?

Here are a few indicators:

- When you do things out of your control, such as being driven
  or feeling compelled.
- When you cannot stop doing things that negatively affect your
  health, family, and work.
- If you are uncomfortable with the actions of called people of
  God.
- When the unnatural becomes natural for you. (This is especially
  true of deviant sexual behavior.)

Perhaps Paul was explaining in Romans the situation he faced without actually commenting about the fact that spirits can both oppress a person from
outside and influence you so strongly from the inside that they have temporary
control over certain types of emotions and feelings, even in Christians. Paul
wrote about this experience as a Christian:

> For what I do is not the good I want to do; no, the evil I do not want to
> do—this I keep on doing. Now if I do what I do not want to do, it is no
> longer I who do it, but it is sin living in me that does it. So I find this
> law at work: When I want to do good, evil is right there with me. For in
> my inner being I delight in God's law; but I see another law at work in
> the members of my body, waging war against the law of my mind and
> making me a prisoner of the law of sin at work within my members.
> What a wretched man I am! Who will rescue me from this body of
> death? Thanks be to God—through Jesus Christ our Lord!"
>
> —ROMANS 7:19–25, NIV

What could Paul mean by "the sin living in me"? Was it merely a pattern
of behavior, feelings, and emotions, or was it a spirit? If he was struggling, as
indicated, perhaps he was explaining something that was so common that he

knew the readers would understand his meaning. It seems he was describing how the driven or compulsive nature of sin has a spirit as its source and that only Jesus can rescue or deliver someone from it.

Some would deny that any other demonic spirit could be in you once Jesus' Spirit dwells within you. However, if the demonic spirit had permission to enter, does Jesus have the right to chase it away without your permission when He comes in? Not really. To believe that every evil spirit will depart automatically when Jesus arrives is merely wishful thinking on your part. Now, if you identify the spirit, you, with the help of Jesus, can command it to leave. But, until you renounce the demon's right to be there and you stop doing whatever gave it the right to take up residence, the demon has the right to be there because he came in through your tacit permission. You will find that as demons are cast out, you become more sensitive to any that might remain. Even after they are gone, you could still carry out emotional patterns out of habit. These have to be changed or else that will be an invitation for the spirit to return.

The principle to remember is that if after seeking the help of Jesus to overcome something that manifests itself in sinful actions or even unhealthy mental states, you cannot change or cease, it is probably a spirit controlling this aspect of your life.

Summary of Major Points

- Jesus knew before He created anything that free will choices were a prerequisite to having faith as well as love for God.
- Jesus also knew that created beings with free will would commit sin and this would cause a separation from God.
- After the fall of the angels, who are now called demons or evil spirits, Satan has the right to exercise power over the earth through them.
- Demons are warring against man by tempting man and manifesting themselves through man. They cause illnesses, both physical and mental, as well as other problems for man, including negative, aggressive emotions.
- Jesus brings deliverance. However, as Christians, we must follow the Holy Spirit's leading and use the weapons provided to us. (See 2 Corinthians 6:7, KJV; 10:4, NKJV; Romans 13:12, KJV.)

?

3

MAN

T HERE IS A path that man's relationship with God has taken. It has changed over the centuries. The history of that relationship demonstrates why we are presently in the Era of Faith, the last era before Jesus returns. He asked His disciples, "When the Son of man comes, will He find faith on the earth?" (Luke 18:8). The path started in the Garden in Eden (Gen. 2:8).

IN THE GARDEN

It has often been the position of religious institutions to blame Eve for succumbing to the temptation of Satan. However, there are several important points that need to be understood.

- Prior to any creation, God knew this would happen (Eph. 3:9–11). Therefore, we need to forget about what would have happened if she had not been tempted. In some manner, it was inevitable that man would sin because he was given free will and he was not perfect.
- God *did not* create evil. It was a byproduct of erroneous free will choices, first by Satan and his followers. God did, however, create a situation that would allow the potential for evil to be made manifest. However, if God merely wanted to prevent evil from being made manifest, He would not have created anything. In evaluating this alternative, He decided to go ahead with creation because of another higher purpose, such as the supremacy of love, faith, and trust in Him.
- In any event, the New Testament writers believed that Eve was the one deceived by Satan. Adam knowingly recognized and ate of the fruit, probably because he did not understand why it did not appear to have any adverse effect on Eve. This assumes

Adam had knowledge of what death meant. In the final analysis, it was Adam's responsibility.

• Moses, the acknowledged initial author of Genesis, states that
the knowledge of good and evil was equal to gaining wisdom. It
is doubted that Eve would have had any concept of wisdom.

There are two common beliefs about the Garden experience that are not
clear. First, did Eve eat of the fruit earlier than Adam did or simultaneously with
Adam? Some versions imply that she first ate and then gave the fruit to Adam.
Others state they were together, so the eating was almost simultaneous.[83]

The second common belief is that she was deceived by Satan, but that Adam
knew he was not supposed to eat of the fruit and did anyway.[84] Thus, Eve was
deceived, but Adam knowingly did what he knew he should not have. (The
Bible does not explain why Adam decided to go against God's instructions.
Clearly, while he had the free will to do it, there were consequences, which
he did not know about.)[85] Both were punished in different ways. Adam would
have to toil rather than just till, tend, or keep the garden for their food (Gen.
3:17–19). Eve would incur pain when having childbirth.

In any event, evil started with Satan, and it was known by God before
Creation that Satan would initiate evil. These events, however, merely set the
stage for the demonstration that faith in God, which also generates a relationship of love and trust, can come from man even though man begins in a state
of sin. He can only accomplish this, however, after he experiences repentance

---

83 Actually, the togetherness that is expressed in some versions is sometimes in the next sentence, so
there could have been some time lapse. It appears clear that Adam does not seem to be nearby while
Satan is convincing Eve that she ought to try the fruit, unless you believe that only Eve understood
the serpent's conversation and Adam was just standing there not aware of what was going on. The
most likely situation is that Eve was alone when she picked the fruit and took a bite. Adam tells God
that Eve gave it to him, thus eliminating the possibility of a joint picking of the fruit. Perhaps the
fruit tasted good and she wanted to share it with Adam. Rather than Eve having her eyes immediately opened to good and evil, she merely wanted Adam to experience the taste.

84 It is recorded that Adam listened to Eve and perhaps accepted her guidance or encouragement to
eat the fruit. This implies that Eve convinced Adam to eat the fruit. (It appears that Adam should
have recognized the fruit. Otherwise, he would not have been directly punished. To Adam's credit,
he did not try the "I forgot" defense.)

85 This is the hidden cost of free will. There are unknown consequences, unknown because we
cannot take into account or see into the future to know all potential impacts from both direct and
indirect consequences of our decisions, nor do we always realize, particularly when our spirit is
immature, that our "self" can manifest its desires to the exclusion of God's.

and invites Jesus into his heart and his spirit is cleansed of sin and reborn through Jesus' presence.

How Has Man's Relationship with God Changed Over Time?

Man's relationship with God is reflected by the progress of history, as recorded in the Bible, as it affected the predecessors and descendants of Abraham, the first man of faith.

- Garden—In our sinless state, man enjoyed the maximum relationship with God while on Earth.

- Garden to the Flood—approximately 1,650 years; called the Era of Traditions; the wickedness of man increases

- The Flood to Abraham—approximately 430 years; wickedness returns

- Abraham to the Exodus—approximately 430 years; a man of faith starts a new era

- The Exodus to Jesus—approximately 1,500 years; the Era of the Law

- Jesus to the present—approximately 1,975 years; the Era of Faith

From the Garden to the Flood— The Era of Traditions[86]

Measuring the passage of time has been possible because God set stars in the sky knowing that man would measure time by them (Gen. 1:16). This is important because modern man questions whether ancient man could measure time accurately because prior to the flood man is recorded as living a long life span. Lives were measured in hundreds of years rather than by decades. The oldest man lived 969 years (Gen. 5:27). He was Methuselah, the grandfather of Noah.

---

86 This was during the age or period where oral history was used as the means to pass down moral standards and beliefs concerning God to successor generations, including what should and should not be done.

Noah's father, Lamech, lived 777 years. Most of the patriarchs lived more than nine hundred years.[87]

These are long periods, but the earth was different then. Namely, there existed a firmament in the heavens. It is unclear what this actually was. Some believe it was an ice layer that blocked harmful radiation from the sun. Whatever it was, it did not prevent people from seeing at least the brightest stars and measuring time by those stars. It is worth noting that while the firmament existed, there is no mention of rain falling in the Bible until the Flood. Plants received their water from a rising water table or streams (Gen. 2:5–6). Note in the graph below that the longevity of man became shorter after the flood.

During this period prior to the Flood when man lived for long periods,[88] humanity, except for a few, became wicked. Moral standards had been orally past down. However, man began to worship demons and spirits, while also falling into every kind of fleshly sin. Man was running wild without any moral compass, and Satan was having his easiest time.

The following graph illustrates the life spans of the early patriarchs and how Adam would have been able to pass on information about his experiences in the Garden of Eden. Notice also how the life spans decreased after the Flood. Men also started having children at a much earlier average age (at approximately thirty-five years old rather than at over one hundred years old).[89]

---

87 Through Noah, seven out of ten patriarchs lived over 900 years. Adam lived 930 years after he was expelled from the garden.

88 To try to explain why man does not live that long today, some people have determined that early man did not know how to measure time, especially years. They have divided the time stated for the ages of the early patriarchs by four, thinking it was really seasons. However, that would conflict with some of those who are recorded as having become a father at a very early age. It would be better to realize that God placed stars in the heavens for man to be able to measure time. Another method would be by lunar months of 29.5 days. A lunar year is only 354 days, so a calendar would catch up every thirty-two years. Thus, even keeping track of time by the moon, the number of years could be high by 3 percent. However, crop cycles are another method of counting time, and it would not let a lunar calendar stray too far off.

89 Perhaps people matured quicker after the Flood. In other words, before the Flood people reached maturity after fifty to sixty years of age. Prior to the flood, the youngest age for starting to have children was sixty-five. After the Flood, they were often around thirty-five years of age when their first child was born.

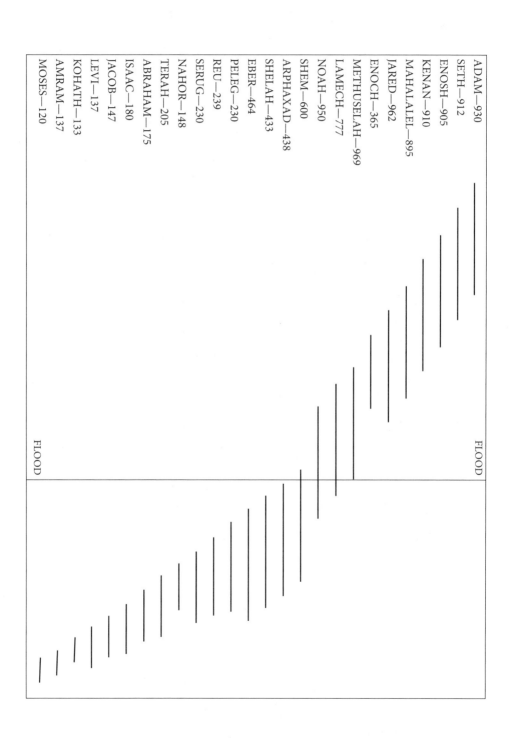

ADAM—930
SETH—912
ENOSH—905
KENAN—910
MAHALALEL—895
JARED—962
ENOCH—365
METHUSELAH—969
LAMECH—777
NOAH—950
SHEM—600
ARPHAXAD—438
SHELAH—433
EBER—464
PELEG—230
REU—239
SERUG—230
NAHOR—148
TERAH—205
ABRAHAM—175
ISAAC—180
JACOB—147
LEVI—137
KOHATH—133
AMRAM—137
MOSES—120

FLOOD

FLOOD

THE FLOOD TO ABRAHAM

Right after the Flood, man often lived as much as six hundred years. However, over this period of approximately 390 years, man's life expectancy drops to approximately two hundred years. During this time, man began worshiping gods of nature. However, God found a man of faith, Abraham. He had eight sons, the most recognized being Isaac from Sarah and Ishmael from Hagar, Sarah's slave-girl.[90]

ABRAHAM TO THE EXODUS

Some of Abraham's offspring were in captivity most of this time period, and they lived under the rule of an Egyptian pharaoh. During this time, they rekindled their love of God and awaited their deliverance from bondage.

THE EXODUS TO JESUS—THE ERA OF LAW

After the people told Moses they wanted laws from God, which He gave them, they promptly began to violate or ignore them. During this interval, man never adopted a faith concept with God but instead wanted to be controlled, insofar as their relationship with God was concerned, by religious laws and regulations and to use good works to offset sins.[91] Thus, man wanted to insure his relationship with God by works of his flesh. In other words, man's salvation was believed to be based upon the concept of justification by good works with the additional use of sacrifices to God as a means to purge oneself from the consequences of sinful behavior. This of course glorifies man, inspires his ego and pride, lifts him up, and does nothing to change the heart.

Thus, once again man demonstrated the basic rebellious nature of man's spirit. Abraham's seed suffered many consequences for their rebellion. However, the main lesson for us is that having laws to follow does nothing to change one's spirit. If they are followed, man is tempted to take pride in himself. Perhaps the reason why man wanted to have laws to follow is that he had a need to overcome the feeling of rejection and separation from God. Many of us point to

---

90 Abraham married Keturah after Sarah died. He had six sons. Perhaps he also had an unspecified number of sons by other concubines (Gen. 25:1).

91 Jewish Law has several parts. The Torah, the first five books of the Bible, contain 613 biblical rules, or mitzvot. The Talmud is made up of oral interpretations of the Torah. The Mishnah is a compilation of legal opinions and debates. *The Law* generally refers to the Ten Commandments and the 613 rules.

our good works while avoiding having to deal with the responsibility for the sin within our spirit.

Finally, however, after approximately fifteen hundred years, man was given the opportunity to move into a faith relationship with God. This was created by Jesus.[92]

Jesus to the Present—The Era of Faith

Prior to Jesus, we were in a reward or punishment system that controlled our relationship with God. The religious leaders prior to Jesus, usually concentrated on the adherence to traditions, laws, or ordinances in making a judgment of what would be acceptable to God, even though God had indicated otherwise through His prophets.[93] Unfortunately, even today, particularly for non-Christians, acceptance by God is believed to be dependent on their actions. For them, life is a test of their ability to control their desires and flesh. God is not perceived as a loving God, but instead as a demanding God who may not be trusted. Perhaps this was because the Bible writers, both Old and New Testament, use the word "fear" so often.[94] A fear of God causes sinners to wake up to their eventual destruction and is the initial step for seeking the truth about God, but one must transcend from merely fear of God into a recognition of His love and His desire for a relationship with us. This step is essential to a relationship with God based on faith.

We are now in an era wherein God is proving that faith, and not rules or law, is what is important. First, only faith affects the spirit, whereas the adherence to the Law tends to affect one's pride. Second, when laws do not specifically

---

92 It is much more difficult to prove or disprove the existence of someone who lived two thousand years ago because the type of records we take for granted today did not exist then. Birth records and other legal documents did not exist. Instead, one has to rely on a variety of sources, usually writings, which tell us about the person. In this case, at least three individuals who knew Jesus wrote about Him. Mark, Matthew, and John knew Him. Luke recorded information passed on orally by others who witnessed His ministry. However, historical proof is of little importance once you have actually had a salvation experience because Jesus proves Himself to you.

93 Psalm 24:4 states that God desires clean hands and a pure heart. (See also Proverbs 20:9.) Second Chronicles 12:14 says that failure to set one's heart on seeking God can cause evil to be manifested. Psalm 51:17 indicates that the true sacrifice to God is a broken spirit—a broken and contrite heart.

94 The Gospels do not indicate that Jesus used that term, except in Luke 12:5. In this verse, He was stating that God, who could destroy body and soul, was more powerful than those that could only destroy the body. Those in sin should realize the situation they are in and perhaps fear the judgment. However, God would not resort to compulsion to achieve that end. It does not appear that any coercion was used against the rebellious or fallen angels.

cover a situation, either directly or indirectly, your spirit influences the choice. If your spirit is conformed into the likeness of God, you will make the right choice. If not, you will make the choice that benefits yourself.

SUMMARY OF MAJOR POINTS

- Jesus knew before Creation that man would sin and that He would have to be the atonement for that sin. Humanity will demonstrate the superiority of faith over the Law. One changes the spirit, the other merely the outward manifestation.
- Man's relationship with God has evolved to its present stage from a period of traditions with no law to a period of laws from God to the final period of faith in which the laws are unnecessary because of the sanctification process on our spirit,[95] created by faith and trust in God and the work of the Holy Spirit. This is the last era, a period in which faith in Jesus brings about the completion of God's plan for all creation.

---

95 The spirit behind the law, in essence, is written into one's heart or spirit, and one becomes what he or she could never accomplish through obedience to the written Law.

4

JESUS

Who was Jesus?

I S IT NECESSARY for our salvation that we understand who Jesus really was? Yes, it is critical that we understand that He was the Son of God, actually part of the Godhead, who created man, and that He came to Earth to become a sacrifice for our sin. He was neither created by God nor adopted as the Son of God some time after His birth.[96] In addition, if we repent of our sin and believe in Him with our heart, His shed blood atones for our sin. Thus, our belief in Him is critical; however, we must also understand who He was. As we do, our love of Him and our relationship with Him becomes stronger.

Jesus came from above, meaning heaven, and He was sent by the Father.

> No one has ever gone into heaven except the One who came from heaven—the Son of man.
>
> —JOHN 3:13[97]

> For God did not send his Son into the world to condemn the world, but to save the world through him. [18]Whoever believes in him is not condemned, but whoever does not believe stands condemned already because he has not believed in the name of God's one and only Son.
>
> —JOHN 3:17–18

---

96 If you do not actually believe in the Trinity, even if you believe you are worshiping God through Jesus, you are not worshipping God. You are worshiping a substitute, something created, and you believe also that Jesus is a liar. Worshiping something created is a violation of the Second Commandment. Thus, unless you believe that Jesus was part of God prior to the Incarnation, you do not actually worship God. If you do not have this level of understanding, then you must believe that Jesus was something created by God or adopted by God and the Jesus you acknowledge has no meaning.

97 Perhaps the title "Son of man" means "the Son of mankind," His creation, because of the human nature in Jesus, the ultimate and perfect man. This was mentioned in Daniel 7:13 (NKJV): "And behold, One like the Son of man, Coming with the clouds of heaven!"

Furthermore, Jesus said, "For I have come down from heaven not to do my will but to do the will of him who sent me" (John 6:38). John the Baptist said, "For the one whom God has sent speaks the words of God, for God gives the Spirit without limit. The Father loves the Son and has placed everything in his hands. Whoever believes in the Son has eternal life, but whoever rejects the Son will not see life, for God's wrath remains on him" (John 3:34–36).

In these and other places in the Bible, it is clearly stated that Jesus was not merely a good person who was sinless and who thus became the Son of God. It was not because Jesus was sinless before being baptized by John the Baptist that God endowed Jesus with extraordinary powers.[98] The Spirit of Jesus preexisted His human form as part of the triune God. He created all things. As part of God's plan to bring about man's salvation through faith in God, He decided to sacrifice Himself as a demonstration of His love and as the only means of atonement for man's sin, for those that believe and have faith in Him.

The human life Jesus lived out was sinless even though He was tested or tempted by Satan.[99] During His mission on Earth, He demonstrated and spoke on the differences between the life of the flesh and the life led by the spirit, in particular, how they conflict and how the spirit must overcome the flesh's desires through faith in the one and only true God. Thus, understanding Jesus and God is critical, namely that God has represented Himself to man as the Father, Son, and Holy Spirit. We must understand as much as we can the breath and depth of God. This only occurs through a relationship with Jesus that begins with a rebirth of our spirit. Unfortunately, if our concept and knowledge of God is incorrect or limited, we have almost no ability to relate with Him. In other words, false concepts will interfere with our ability to know and trust Him. Thus, it is important that we personally know Jesus, not merely know what Jesus said.

---

98 We know little of Jesus prior to the baptism by John, except for the time He spent in the temple at age twelve. If the events of his life were supposed to be imitated, we would have been furnished those guidelines.

99 Satan never really had any likelihood that he could convince Jesus to accept his proposals because Jesus had the mind of the Father because the Father was within Him (Matt. 11:27; John 10:15, 38). Besides, before Creation, His incarnation and death were part of God's plans, and Jesus knew this from the beginning. He indirectly confirmed He knew His purpose when He was twelve when He was asked by his parents why He had left them. He said to them, "Why were you searching for me? Didn't you know I had to be in my Father's house?" (Luke 2:49).

JESUS AND THE TRINITY IN THE ERA OF FAITH

We are in the Era of Faith. Because of this, Jesus *did not* succinctly state, "The Father, the Holy Spirit, and I are the one and only true God. We have always been and will always be God, although for a short time I have taken on the form of man. This was done so that I may be the sacrifice as the atonement for sin, for all who believe and have faith in me, so they may have eternal life with us in the kingdom of God. Those who reject me will be sent to hell."

If Jesus had made a statement like the one above, most theological issues would have been reduced down to whether you accept His complete statement or merely parts of it as truth; whether you would believe it to be completely untrue; or an exaggeration by the writers, trying to push their own agenda. It would have eliminated the issue of whether He was created or adopted by God. On the other hand, it may have been too much for people to immediately accept or understand. Thus, the substance or concepts contained in the statement would come to us piecemeal, requiring faith to accept.

The use of the term *trinity* was developed long after the gospels were written. As you would expect, the Bible does not contain anything that would rebut the concept of the Trinity, and it also does not contain any succinct statement explaining it. Jesus does not even mention the Father, the Son (Jesus), and the Holy Spirit in the same sentence, except when Jesus gives His commission to His disciples to baptize in those names (Matt. 28:19). We understand the concept of the Trinity after conceptually merging the statements Jesus made, as well as those of the writers of the New Testament. After accepting Jesus as your Savior, the next step is to accept who He really is—a part of the Trinity. If you cannot, then you will not know God.

THE PURPOSE OF JESUS IN THE ERA OF FAITH

Jesus came to fulfill the Law and Prophets (Matt. 5:17–18; 7:12).

(See also the following verses, which indicate Jesus came from and was sent by the Father.)

- John 1:2–5, 10, 14, 18, 29
- John 6:38–40
- John 8:42
- John 10:9
- John 12:49–50
- John 16:5
- Luke 4:43

All that belongs to the Father also belongs to Jesus.

- John 17:20–23
- Matthew 11:27
- Luke 10:22
- Luke 22:29

The judgment of man will be made by Jesus.

- John 5:22, 30
- 2 Corinthians 5:10

Salvation is only through Jesus.

- John 1:12–13
- John 3:5–8, 14, 16–18, 36
- John 4:42
- John 5:23–25, 39–40
- John 6:33, 38–40, 51
- John 10:9, 28
- John 14:6–7
- Matthew 7:14

If we know Jesus, we can enter into the kingdom of God. However, those that merely recognize Jesus as Lord will not actually enter the kingdom of heaven (Matt. 7:21–23). Even if they were used by God to perform miracles, they still will not enter the kingdom of heaven. Therefore, you must know Jesus, and He must know you.[100] Paul said belief in Jesus must be in your heart (Rom. 10:9–10). Thus, mental assent, patterns, or habits from childhood are not enough. Faith comes from your heart (Matt. 8:13; Mark 11:23). However, hindrances can occur in the process and various things can cause diversions and stumbling blocks (Matt. 14:31; 21:21).

Naturally, you cannot take the Law and attempt to modify it with Christian principles, creating a mixture, and expect to achieve salvation. There needs to be a new container created, a new or reborn spirit (Luke 5:36–39). Jesus came to provide the means to achieve a reborn spirit.

---

100 Knowing Jesus means having an intimate relationship with Him, not just knowledge of facts concerning the historical Jesus.

First, Jesus Proves Himself

What were the miracles?[101]

1. Visions of distant events
   John 1:48

2. Changes the nature of matter
   John 2:7–8

3. Foretells the future
   John 13:38
   Luke 9:44; 19:30–31; 22:10–12, 32
   Matthew 21:2; 26:2, 34
   Mark 11:2–4; 14:9, 13

4. Calms a storm
   Luke 8:23–24
   Matthew 8:26

5. Raised the dead to life again
   Mark 5:39–42[102]
   John 11:38–44
   Matthew 11:5
   Luke 7:14; 8:54

6. Tells fishermen where to catch fish
   Luke 5:4

7. Causes a coin to appear in a fish's mouth
   Matthew 17:27

8. Knows people's thoughts
   Matthew 9:4; 12:25
   Luke 5:22–24; 9:47; 11:17

---

101 The citations from different Gospels sometimes may be recording the same event. Mark's Gospel is currently considered, but not conclusively proven, to have been the first written Gospel. Matthew and Luke may have also had additional sources, perhaps oral, perhaps written. Luke, in particular, writes about things not covered in the other Gospels. For that matter, there is the likelihood that oral recitation from observers was also relied upon, even for Mark and Matthew. Note that Matthew and Luke had a different focus, objective, or audience.

102 The girl's parents and others believed the girl had died. Perhaps it had occurred just before Jesus arrived. It could have been that He did not want it known at that time by the girl's father, who was the local synagogue ruler, that Jesus had the power to raise the dead.

9. Knows personal information about strangers
   John 4:17–18
   Luke 19:5

10. Drove out spirits (demons)
    Luke 4:35, 41; 6:18; 8:2, 33
    Matthew 8:16, 32; 12:22
    Mark 1:34, 39; 5:13; 16:9

11. Delegated power to others, even Judas[103]
    Matthew 10:8
    Mark 3:13–15; 6:7–13; 16:17
    Luke 9:1–6; 10:17–19

12. Jesus knew of His coming betrayal, death, and resurrection
    Mark 9:31; 10:33–34
    Luke 9:22; 18:31–33
    Matthew 17:9; 20:19
    John 6:70

13. Touching His cloak brought healing if faith was there
    Mark 5:28–29; 6:56
    Luke 8:44
    Matthew 14:36

14. Unnamed miraculous signs
    John 2:23

15. Leprosy
    Mark 1:40–42
    Luke 17:13–19[104]
    Matthew 11:5

16. Healing and deliverance from afar off
    Luke 7:3–10; 17:14
    John 4:50
    Matthew 15:28
    Mark 7:29

---

103 Even without specific authority from Jesus, others cast out demons in His name (Luke 9:49; 11:19; Mark 9:38–41). However, having demons under your command is not sufficient. You must know Jesus to be saved (Matt. 7:22–23).

104 This miracle was unusual in that they obeyed Him without an outward sign that they had been healed. The healing did not occur until they were walking to the temple to show themselves to the priest.

17. Deaf, dumb, and blind healed, lame walk
    Matthew 9:30; 11:5; 20:34; 21:14
    Luke 11:14
    Mark 8:23–25
    Mark 7:32–36

18. Walks on water
    Mark 6:45–51
    John 6:19
    Matthew 14:25–26

19. Feeds four thousand men, plus women and children
    Mark 8:6–9
    Matthew 15:32–38

20. Feeds five thousand men, plus women and children
    Mark 6:39–44
    Luke 9:13–17
    John 6:10–11
    Matthew 14:14–21

21. Fig tree withers from curse
    Matthew 21:19
    Mark 11:14

22. Missing body parts made whole[105]
    Matthew 15:30

23. Healed all the sick
    Matthew 8:16; 9:35; 12:15
    Luke 4:40

24. Shriveled hand
    Matthew 12:13
    Mark 3:5
    Luke 6:10

25. Dropsy (excessive, harmful water retention)
    Luke 14:4

---

105 Jesus restored healthy, operating body parts to those who lacked them. This event refutes any argument that the problem was a psychosomatic one. One should give the people of two thousand years ago some credit. They were not gullible, stupid, or ignorant people. They knew when they were blind or deaf. They may have believed that sin was often the cause of their problem, at least according to the priests, but their problems were not imaginary.

26. Blind Bartimaeus
    Mark 10:51–52
    Luke 18:35–43

27. Boy with seizures
    Mark 9:19–26
    Luke 9:39–41

28. Rebukes the fever in Peter's mother-in-law
    Luke 4:39

29. Crippled back
    Luke 13:11–13

It is likely that Jesus healed many other people with many different types of problems that are not specifically recorded in John's Gospel but rather fall within a general statement that He healed them all. It is doubtful that over an approximate three-year period the specifics of every particular healing could be remembered. Undoubtedly, there were multiple healings of the same problem, such as blindness, and many were healed when the problem was not stated. They may not have even used terms like *cancer*.

It is clear, however, that Jesus had authority over all creation, including matter, flesh, and spirit. He knew past and future events, as well as people's thoughts, both in the present and in the past. To bring about the culmination of God's plan for all creation, all necessary authority, knowledge, and power resided in Him, even in His human nature.

Jesus' love was so great that He laid down His life for those who believe in Him.[106] Because of this, those who believe are saved and will be with God throughout the remainder of eternity. There are no optional methods for man's salvation. There is no other path except through Him. To argue or seek any other means for salvation demeans God's plan. In addition, God makes the rules, not us. All previous paths for righteousness or salvation have been subsumed by Jesus' plan.

---

106 Jesus said, "Greater love has no one than this, than to lay down one's life for his friends. You are My friends if you do whatever I command you" (John 15:13–14, NKJV).

WHICH MIRACLE WAS FIRST?

The miracle of Jesus turning water into wine is often mentioned as the first recorded miracle. This is only recorded by John (John 2:9).[107] The fact that Jesus told Mary that His hour had not yet come is often taken to mean it was to be his first recorded miracle. However, that is merely speculation, because He could have also been talking about the first miracle in the area of Cana, in Galilee. Matthew records what appears to have been an earlier miracle in Jesus' ministry, one that took place soon after the temptation experience, when Jesus healed a man with leprosy (Matt. 8:3).

MIRACLES TODAY

Today, healings are still being manifested. Most are occurring through the medical profession. Before man was created, God decided that man should have a certain amount of intelligence, and over time and often by the inspiration of God, man would discover how creation functioned and interacts. Thus, medical information has been discovered or developed concerning humanity that has benefitted man. Therefore, even without a direct miracle, God is able to help humanity overcome the effects of the environment and Satan through the hands of men.

One must conclude that at the very least God has created opportunities for medical cures that would have been unavailable hundreds of years ago. Thus, today we may take for granted a healing that would have once required direct intervention by God. Nevertheless, healings brought about by medical science are a blessing from God and we should be thankful.[108]

---

107 When this event occurred is not clear. While John said it was on the third day (John 2:1), it was probably not the third day of the first year of ministry. It could have meant there was a break, perhaps over the winter, and this event occurred on the third day of the second year of Jesus' ministry. This would explain why there is no mention of Jesus' time of temptation by Satan in John's Gospel. Had there been no miracles the first year? If there had been, it would explain why Mary was so confident that Jesus would solve the problem of not enough wine. On the other hand, if this was indeed the first year, then Jesus had probably performed other miracles before His baptism by John that Mary was privy to but are otherwise not recorded.

108 However, when God directly intervenes, there are no side affects. When He heals, it is perfect. Thus, not all medicine is the result of God inspiring someone. Many times—perhaps most of the time—it is merely man's understanding of how the body functions and interacts with both natural and synthetic chemicals. It is difficult to distinguish God's benefit for humanity from man's intellectual abilities, but the general concept and relationship between illnesses and cures was built into the creative effort of God. Thus, God is still and always will be the ultimate Healer. His healing is always perfect.

Some people believe in the supernatural intervention by God as the only means of medical treatment that should be sought. This, in a way, ignores what God has already provided and is therefore presumptive. If you believe that medical science is from Satan, you misunderstand Satan. Satan is not in the business of helping humanity. To be sure, prayer for healing is necessary.[109] However, we have a responsibility to do what we can using what God has already provided. Life has its problems, which shapes us to some extent. Prayer to God should not be something that is merely habit or a last resort but rather something our spirit should know when to do. Prayer brings us the knowledge of the will of God about the situation. The reality is, as we live life our spirit should be ready for that moment of closeness with God.

Concerning prayer, Jesus gives these two examples. In Luke 11:9–10, Jesus says, "I say to you: Ask and it will be given to you; seek and you will find; knock and the door will be opened to you.[10] For everyone who asks receives; he who seeks finds; and to him who knocks, the door will be opened." This statement should not be taken as a blanket, unconditional promise. Jesus also said in Luke 18:6–8, "Listen to what the unjust judge says. And will not God bring about justice for his chosen ones, who cry out to him day and night? Will he keep putting them off? I tell you, he will see that they get justice, and quickly. However, when the Son of Man comes, will he find faith on the earth?" The underlying condition or premise of each is faith. In addition, faith comes after God has spoken to you concerning your prayer.[110] Once God has spoken, it is merely a matter of time before His answer is manifest. Naturally, our faith must be maintained until the time of manifestation.

---

109   God has sovereign jurisdiction over healings and miracles. He is not under an obligation to heal us just because we believe He should or will because we are His children. We certainly cannot be presumptive or ever believe that we have a right to be healed. Thus, we must take advantage of the medical science, even though it is not perfect. However, God is not the last resort, He is the first. First, we go to Him. However, sometimes we conclude that a tragedy was God's will; or, if we have prayed about a situation, that it was our lack of faith that failed to change the situation. What we are called to do is pray, with faith, that God hears our requests, even though He is already fully aware of the situation. He is a God of love and compassion. We must recognize that God doesn't change His mind and that we must seek His will. (See 1 John 5:13–15.) He will respond to us, if our spirit is open to His will for the situation. We must also remember that God has His purposes. The lack of an immediate remedy is not always because of our lack of faith but rather because of our lack of knowing His will.

110   Persistence in prayer builds faith by causing you to focus and become earnest. In other words, this causes you to hear God in your spirit, which in turn makes your spirit more sensitive to Him. (Faith will be discussed in more detail in Chapter 8.)

What Is the Relevance of the Law?[111]

What was Jesus' position?

What did Jesus mean when He said He came to fulfill the Law? How is the Law fulfilled? Perhaps it simply means to move from an era of discipline of the flesh and measuring righteousness by how successful one is, to an era of faith and the sanctification and maturing of our spirit. See the table below.

Commandment	Action Involved	Spiritual Issue
1	Have no other gods[†]	Pride
2	Do not have or worship idols	Pride
3	Do not misuse the Lord's name	Pride and love
4	Remember the Sabbath	Pride
5	Honor your father and mother (See Eph. 6:1–6.)	Pride
6	Do not murder[‡]	Love
7	Do not commit adultery	Pride
8	Do not steal	Greed
9	Do not give false testimony	Lying
10	Do not covet, or feel an inordinate desire for, anything of your neighbor's	Greed

[†] One may believe that there is a God, but that doesn't mean He is your God. Is it a personal relationship? Jesus is the only avenue of establishing a personal relationship with the true God.

[‡] The original King James Version used the word *kill*, while the New King James Version and most other versions use *murder*. Using the term *kill* produces inconsistencies, because God said that a person who shed blood would have his blood shed (Gen. 9:6). The concern in this commandment is with innocent blood being intentionally shed (Prov. 6:17).

You will notice in the table above that fleshly activities usually have an underlying spiritual issue.[112] If one's spirit is right, one will not carry out these fleshly activities. Thus, one must move from the Law and its legalistic principles

---

111 What has been called the Law comes from the first five books of the Old Testament, also called the Pentateuch or Torah. It is believed to have been initially authored by Moses but revised over the centuries. It contains, among many other things, 613 laws, commandments, and ordinances that cover a broad spectrum of Jewish life.

112 There are often multiple issues involved. Some are derived from pride, such as lust and envy. A common one is the kingdom of self. Individuals operating in the kingdom of self focus primarily on their needs and desires as being the most important in their existence. Thus, they cannot consider being subjected to any authority over their spirit. While their flesh may be subject to outside authority, their spirit is not, and they sit on their own throne.

concerning the flesh into the spiritual principles that influence our spirit. Put another way, we change emphasis from controlling our outer man to changing the inner man by a purification of our spirit. However, this difficult task is only accomplished by starting with a rebirth of our spirit and then traveling along a narrow path that matures our spirit with the help of Jesus and the Holy Spirit.[113]

Pride, or self, is a major cause of our violation of God's ten commandments. The second is our failure to love. The third is greed. The fourth is our disregard for truth. Pride can be both obvious and very subtle. It will attempt to ignore or diminish the one true God. It will attempt to replace God. The replacement can be a subtle substitution caused by the idolization of people, things, systems, or intellect. Any imagine created by man that is said to represent God, diminishes God.[114] Things such as homes, cars, your family, your body, fame, success, money, or power can all become idols that diminish God, because they become your primary focus as an extension of self. Pride can interfere with observing the Sabbath if we do not use it as a day of rest and a time to be with God.[115] Can we ever pray effectively without a humble spirit?

Many of the prohibitions in the Ten Commandments are directly a result of man's pride. However, by changing our spirit, we would not even think about violating the Commandments. This is how the Law is fulfilled. Only Jesus can accomplish this. However, during our movement along the path to spiritual maturity, we sometimes want to fall back or rely on the Law because we are comfortable with it. However, doing so has the subtle effect of deceiving ourselves into thinking we are making progress with our spirit when we have merely learned to control our flesh. This is particularly true if we focus on performing good works in the belief that they will offset our sins. That does

---

113 Some people are Christians, but they still have an evil heart. This can occur because of the influence of evil spirits still within them. They fail to make any progress on the path of sanctification and maturity.

114 Aaron took gold from the Israelites and fashioned an idol in the shape of a calf. When Moses asked him what was going on, Aaron said it was a representation of God. God cannot be represented by anything. Our attempt to do so only diminishes Him. Art in churches does not represent God. However, icons, statutes, and the like, if believed to be a replacement of God, would violate the Second Commandment. There is also a more subtle means of idolatry. That is, being a member of a "church" that does not worship the true God. For example, if your belief and faith is not that Jesus is a part of the Trinity, then you do not worship God. You worship a substitute if you believe God created Jesus or adopted Him at some point in His life.

115 Christians should observe the Sabbath. The Sabbath rest is mentioned in 1 Corinthians 16:2 and Revelation 1:10. It was also mentioned over 1,800 years ago by early Christian writers. It is the day of the week Jesus was resurrected.

not work. What adds to the difficulty of separating the spiritual from the flesh is that laws are known and success or failure is easily measured. To complicate the matter even more, Satan and his demons are doing battle with us. Thus, the application of spiritual principles that change our inner man is not always easy or immediately noticeable to us. However, we must not give up, and we must change from the inside.

Jesus said that we must love God with all our heart, soul, and mind. In addition, love your neighbor as yourself (Matt. 22:37–40). These are not an alternative to Jesus. For one thing, you cannot love God with all your heart unless you have a cleansed heart, something only Jesus can cause to happen. How is this accomplished? It is accomplished over a lifetime, beginning with the new birth experience of receiving salvation and then moving through the Baptism with the Holy Spirit, and on to the sanctification process.[116]

Are there deadly sins?

Because sins of the spirit are difficult to address, religious leaders prefer to speak about the various activities that have definitive names, such as *avarice*, *sloth, gluttony, pride,* and *envy,* among others. There is the belief that these are deadly sins that will lead to your destruction in hell. However, while the root cause can be a problem, Jesus only indicated that blasphemy of the Holy Spirit was unforgivable. Paul stated that, "The acts of the sinful nature are obvious: sexual immorality, impurity and debauchery; idolatry and witchcraft; hatred, discord, jealousy, fits of rage, selfish ambition, dissensions, factions and envy; drunkenness, orgies, and the like. I warn you, as I did before, that those who live like this will not inherit the kingdom of God" (Gal. 5:19–21). He also said, "No immoral, impure or greedy person—such a man is an idolater—has any inheritance in the kingdom of Christ and of God" (Eph. 5:5). Notice that the sins listed by Paul involve a spirit issue, just like the so-called deadly sins, which means there is a sin of the heart, or spirit, that needs to be repented of. Repentance involves the cessation of wrong behavior, even those ingrained habits that we would consider as normal. After repenting, you should no longer cling to those desires, habits, and thought patterns. Instead, reject them, confess them to Jesus, repent, and Jesus will forgive us and change our

---

116 Salvation does not mean merely a mental acceptance in Jesus as your Savior because of His sacrifice. That is just the beginning, perhaps the first step. However, it must move into your heart, your spirit. Once that happens, eventually the phrase "believing in Jesus" really does not adequately describe your experience. It becomes a relationship with Jesus that becomes as real as breathing. It becomes something you know, as a fact, not merely a belief. Until then, experiencing the baptism with the Holy Spirit is unlikely because you will lack the necessary faith.

desires (1 John 1:9). Some of these, if influenced or controlled by a demonic spirit, will require your deliverance. Clearly, after your death, you cannot bring these desires into the kingdom of God.

SUMMARY OF MAJOR POINTS

- Jesus, prior to the Incarnation, was set apart by God. Jesus created all that was created knowing that He would need to sacrifice Himself for man.
- Jesus demonstrated His dominion and power over all matter, all flesh, all spirits, and even death. He knew before Creation that religious spirits in certain men would lead them to demand His death.
- After a period of approximately 1,500 years under the Law, Jesus came to fulfill the Law by another means, faith in Him, because the Law did not purify or change a person's spirit.
- The Bible does not say that when you die, your spirit is automatically and completely cleansed or renewed from sin.[117] Therefore, it is incumbent upon you not only to be saved but also to purge yourself of sins of the spirit. One of, if not the biggest, is pride. This pride is unrelated to self-esteem, which recognizes who you are in Jesus. Instead, it is thinking you are better than others are as well as rebelliousness before God. The next is greed, which causes an individual to put him or herself first. When one struggles with greed, his or her needs and desires become all important, and one's primary goal is to satisfy those desires, even if it means lying, stealing, or killing another. The baptism with the Holy Spirit and the sanctification process will aid in the purging of sins of the spirit.

---

117 Not every negative activity or feeling is sinful. You may have a spirit of rejection, but you may not be mean-spirited. You may not actually commit any sins because of this spirit. However, you do miss many opportunities in your relationship with Jesus and other people.

5

BECOMING A CHRISTIAN

Why Become a Christian?

VIL IS IN the world by and through Satan. We are all sinners, and the propensity for evil is within us.[118] You cannot overcome evil by positive mental attitudes or even by controlling your flesh's activities. Your heart remains at least partly evil so long as your spirit is impure. In addition, although God loves all people, you cannot have an eternal relationship with God if you are still a sinner. Sin can only be removed from our hearts by a rebirth or cleansing of our spirit. Because of Jesus' sacrifice, if we repent of the sin and become His children, we are saved from hell. We cannot come to Him with pride in our heart. We have to come to Him as a child, open and without pride. Only He, because He is God, can cleanse us of sin so we may interact with Him.

Salvation—being saved—is not an intellectual experience. It involves a rebirth of your spirit (heart).[119] It is something that only Jesus can cause to take place. Thus, becoming a Christian is a spiritual experience. It is not enough for you to be intellectually convinced, because you must be willing to believe and accept Him into your heart. Before that experience can occur, you have to give up your pride and be willing to risk opening yourself and being vulnerable to Jesus. Only if you lower your guard and invite Him in can He actually enter.

Jesus will not force Himself upon you. Instead, you have to open the door to your heart. Clearly then, believing with your heart is the only thing that counts. (See Romans 10:9.) An intellectual belief or acceptance is not good enough. You could delude yourself your entire life by thinking that your mental belief will save you, but when confronted at the time of judgment, He will deny knowing you. For example, see Matthew 7:21–23, where Jesus said one can even do the

---

118 The "default" place where sinners will spend eternity after their death is hell. Hell, at the very least, is a place of separation from God and a place of punishment. Having a saving knowledge of and relationship with Jesus Christ is the only means of avoiding hell.

119 You are spirit, soul, and flesh (1 Thess. 5:23).

miraculous through the power of God and still be deceived about his or her salvation.

WHAT DOES SALVATION MEAN?

Salvation simply means being saved from hell, the destination of all sinners after their death. There are two places our spirits will dwell for the remainder of eternity, either hell with Satan or heaven with God.[120] The righteous will spend eternity in heaven. Salvation is part of the process of becoming righteous. For the last two thousand-plus years, there has been only one way or path to achieving that status—through Jesus!

Before you can understand salvation, you must first understand who you are.

- You are a son of Adam (Rom. 5:12, 17, 19). You are a sinner by birth as well as by your actions, and the state of your spirit.
- You are condemned to die because of sin, and you will, because of sin, go to hell. (John 3:18).
- When you repent of sin and have faith in Jesus, you become a son of God (John 1:12; Rom. 8:14; Gal. 4:1–5).[121]

Jesus came to establish a new kingdom built upon a relationship with Him. It is known as the kingdom of God. However, it is made up of millions of parts with each one of us having or being a part of it. It does not have a physical dimension.[122] Rather, it is manifested within us. However, when Jesus returns it will become manifested as a visible reality to us. Now we only have glimpses of it within others. Later, after Jesus' return, the kingdom of God will be merged together with that part that is in heaven, and God, at the end, will be "all in all" (1 Cor. 15:28). Salvation through Jesus is the only way to enter into that kingdom.

There are some underlying facts that will help you to understand salvation.

God is unchangeable. First, He is not subject to time. He created it. Second, His character is goodness and perfection. Thus, He does not have any need to

---

120 Jesus and other New Testament writers spoke and wrote about hell. (See Matthew 10:28; 18:9; 23:33; Luke 16:23; 2 Peter 2:4.) Though the term *Sheol* is used most often in the Old Testament, Psalm 9:17 says, "The wicked shall be turned into hell" (KJV).

121 Sons of God have unlimited access to God to fulfill His purposes.

122 We often think of a kingdom as having physical boundaries. In the kingdom of God, there are no outer boundaries, but it is made up of the combination of individual parts in each Christian as well as in heaven.

change, because all things were known to Him before He created anything. When man perceives God as changing, he is wrong. God responds to creation's choices and changes. However, these responses were already known before Creation began.

God established patterns that are revealed in the Bible. However, the Old Testament patterns were limited by the circumstances of man's revelation of God. (See 1 Corinthians 10:1–6; Heb. 8:5–6; 10:1.) God's Word is absolute. However, our understanding of the revelation of the Word will be expanded by the maturity of our spirit (not our intellectual maturity, which is acquired by mental absorption of information and data).

God loves us, and He is concerned about us. We are now, since Jesus' sacrifice and resurrection, in an era of faith, no longer in bondage to the Law. It is critical, however, that you understand that your belief and faith in Jesus must come from your heart, or spirit.[123] When one first believes in his mind, it is sometimes merely a confidence in a statement or promise being made. The mental belief can become faith if it moves into your heart. However, you must want or desire it, not merely accept it, if it is going to change you. As stated elsewhere, believing in your heart is not the same as a mental assent or acceptance. When this is achieved with a humble spirit, the door to your heart can be opened and Jesus can be invited into your heart. Jesus, as well as the Holy Spirit, then begins to abide in you. This has the potential of changing your spirit through the process of sanctification and maturing.

When under the Law, rules and religious laws condemn man. They cannot and will not bring anyone closer to God, even if followed exactly. This is because we will become prideful about our sense of perfection. As a consequence, we will lift ourselves up and consider ourselves better or more deserving of God's blessings.[124] This is just the opposite of what God desires. He wants a heart that is humble before Him, trusts Him, and loves Him beyond measure.

Salvation brings you into a relationship with God that allows His grace and forgiveness to be applied to your repentant and humble spirit. However, we must be ourselves before God. It is foolish to attempt to hide anything from God. Worthiness and guilt are not issues after repentance, because we are all initially unworthy. God's love, through faith in Jesus, helps us overcome these feelings about our self. However, we only become worthy because He has made

---

123 This may, perhaps be explained, as a belief that is at the center or core of your "self". It becomes a belief that is as strong as the belief of your own existence.

124 However, failure in any point of the Law is equal to failure of all of it (James 2:10).

us so. We can never make ourselves worthy. Neither can we ever justify our self to God.

If salvation were dependent on our own merit as measured against our full compliance with rules and laws then we would become our own judge. In essence, we would become a god unto ourselves. Also, Satan will take any opportunity to use our failure to fully comply with every aspect of the rules and laws to attack us and create a sense of rejection, guilt, despair, and discouragement. That is why the Law kills your spirit.

Salvation is only the beginning of the Christian experience. There is the baptism with the Holy Spirit and the sanctification and maturing experience, also known as the baptism with fire, which will be explained later.

WATER BAPTISM

Water baptism is a vital outward act that confirms our salvation to Satan and to the world. It also closes any door of doubt that Satan might use to attack us. Water baptism is an outward sign or ritual that relates to our repentance of sin and symbolizes the beginning of our reborn spirit.

Water baptism is not, however, the normal means of conferring the baptism with the Holy Spirit, even when the Trinity's name is invoked as a blessing on us. (The baptism with the Holy Spirit will be discussed in greater detail in Chapter 6.) That experience has certain prerequisites discussed elsewhere. It is not automatic because the experience has to be understood and desired. In other words, you might believe that it will occur at the time of your water baptism, but usually it will not without meeting a few additional conditions.[125]

Water baptism is a symbol, an ordinance, and a command of Jesus (Matt. 28:18–20), performed after the age of accountability. The method is not critical, but if adequate water is available, immersion is preferred as a symbolic representation of the death of the old self. Jesus said that unless a man has been born of water and spirit, he cannot enter the kingdom of God (John 3:5). John also wrote that the Spirit, water, and blood testify as to our

---

125 Some Christian denominations do not believe it is a separate event, like it was in the early church, although those events mentioned in Acts stated that the participants were speaking in tongues. It is not a mandatory event. Thus, there may be no immediate outward manifestation. More is required of the participant if there is no immediate manifestation. It merely means they have not relinquished the control of their tongue to the Holy Spirit. It will occur later if they want it.

conversion (1 John 5:8).[126] On the day of Pentecost, about three thousand new converts were baptized with water (Acts 2:41). Thus, it was critical that believers repent and be baptized with water for the forgiveness of sin, in the name of Jesus, that they might also receive the gift of the Holy Spirit.[127] Water baptism does not confer salvation. It is, however, a statement to the community and church. It is not a mystical act conferring power.

Baptism with the Holy Spirit is usually a separate event because people usually have already been saved and experienced Jesus' presence, before they come to desire an even greater and deeper relationship with God.

OBSTACLES TO ACCEPTING JESUS AS YOUR SAVIOR

- Ego or pride[128]
- Procrastination
- Confusion
- False security (believing that God would not send people to hell)
- A sense of hopelessness or unworthiness
- Satan[129]
- Trusting in wealth (Mark 10:25)

---

126 John's Gospel; the letters that make up 1, 2, and 3 John; and Revelation were written in the late 80s to mid 90s. They were the last letters to be written by John and appear to be in response to earlier writings as well as the Gnostic movement. It is unknown if he actually wrote them or used an assistant.

127 While it is not clear, Acts 2:41 does not say these three thousand received the baptism with the Holy Spirit. When those in the house were baptized with the Holy Spirit, they spoke in tongues such that many different peoples with different native languages heard their own language. Approximately sixteen different groups of people heard their native tongue. It is possible those individuals spoke different languages or it may have been that they all spoke the same language, which each listener was able to understand as his own native language (Acts 2:6–11).

128 See Luke 18:14.

129 Satan always has a counterfeit movement. In addition, if necessary, he will create a close appearance to God's actual plan. He can even appear as an angel (2 Cor. 11:14). This is one of the reasons that God does not delegate all revelation to come from one person. (The Bible had approximately forty authors over a 1,500-year period.) Usually, when an angel of the Lord brought a message, it was to an individual and it concerned that individual. After Jesus came, there was no longer any need for new doctrine that does not find its foundation in the Bible. Revelation from the Holy Spirit to individuals continues today, but it will never change or conflict with Jesus' message.

CAN YOU BECOME UNSAVED?

You can walk away from your salvation.[130] Paul says to stand fast in our faith and that if one walks away from Him and tries to come back, it is like putting Jesus on the cross again. The term *reprobate* is often used to mean those who have walked away (Rom. 1:28, KJV; 2 Tim. 3:8, KJV; Titus 1:16, KJV). Peter also speaks of those that turn back to the old ways (2 Pet. 2).

Acts that can lead to reprobation:

- once having access to truth, you prostitute it[131]
- acting willfully against God and/or the truth of God
- taking advantage of the innocent
- leading others into rebellious thoughts and acts

Jesus said that blasphemy of the Holy Spirit was an unpardonable sin (Matt. 12:31–32). We would like to believe that no one would walk away from Jesus. However, Jesus said, "No one, having put his hand to the plow, and looking back, is fit for the kingdom of God" (Luke 9:62, NKJV). In addition, according to the writer of Hebrews, it is possible to walk away, particularly for those who are not well grounded and/or mature (Heb. 6:4–6). If one has experienced the baptism with the Holy Spirit, it is less likely. It should be clear, however, that this is something that might not be noticeable to us. Indeed Jesus said that at the time of judgment, even some who had done many things in the name of Jesus would be turned away from heaven because Jesus did not know them (Matt. 7:21–23). Therefore, based upon outward manifestations they appear in sheep's clothing, but they are evil in their heart, even though performing good works.

SUMMARY OF MAJOR POINTS

- Salvation brings us into a right relation with God. The period of Law, which proved ineffectual in changing man's spirit, was replaced by a period of faith in God's Son, Jesus. Salvation can

---

130 Some argue that those that walk away were not really Christians in their heart. However, in 2 Timothy 3:8 and 2 Corinthians 13:5, Paul appears to indicate otherwise.

131 It is possible for a person to find excuses and justifications for committing certain sins to the point that the mind is seared. It will no longer recognize the sin for what it really is. In that, the truth about the sin becomes prostituted. In other words, it is no longer sin in your mind or heart. If not sin to you, you can no longer obtain forgiveness.

only occur by a belief and trust in Jesus Christ, the resurrected Son of God who died as the atonement for our sins.

- Initially, our introduction to Jesus might only involve a mental acceptance. However, that is not enough. The acceptance must become a matter or belief of our heart. Once we begin to believe in our heart, we open the door for Jesus to enter. With Him, the Holy Spirit also becomes a comforter and teacher.
- There is more to being a Christian than being saved by the blood of Jesus. There are other levels of interaction with God. The first is the baptism with the Holy Spirit.
- There is also the sanctification and maturing process guided by the Holy Spirit, called baptism with fire.

6

BAPTISM WITH THE HOLY SPIRIT

B APTISM WITH THE Holy Spirit[132] is an extremely important step in the maturing process of a Christian. The baptism was promised by Jesus and it allows a greater manifestation of the Holy Spirit through us. It is also is a witness of the kingdom of God that is in you (Acts 1:4–8). Without the experience, one will make very slow and difficult progress during the sanctification and maturing process because one lacks the weapons to conduct spiritual warfare. With salvation alone, you can make a great deal of progress, particularly in controlling many sinful flesh activities, but without the baptism with the Holy Spirit, you often lack the ability to distinguish between flesh and underlying problems of the spirit. In many cases, believers who have not experienced the baptism with the Holy Spirit may not be able to determine when an evil spirit is causing certain negative emotions.

WHY IS THE BAPTISM WITH THE HOLY SPIRIT AN ISSUE FOR SOME?

Some Christians have a problem with the subject of the baptism with the Holy Spirit. They believe that it was something that died out after the first or second generation of the early church. Others believe that they were baptized with the Holy Spirit when they were baptized with water because the person ministering the ritual invoked the name of the Holy Spirit.

The latter group believes that there needs to be no separate and distinct

---

132 Jesus used the term *baptized*. (See Acts 1:5.) Luke used various terms, as does the Book of Acts (Acts 2:4, "filled with"; Acts 10:44, NKJV, "fell upon;" and Acts 19:6, NKJV, "came upon"). All spoke in tongues afterwards. However, that is not mandatory criteria, an automatic occurrence, or the only evidence of the baptism with the Holy Spirit.

authority granted, or invitation made, to the Holy Spirit, as a separate event.[133] At the time of salvation, Jesus and the Holy Spirit enter into us. However, the baptism with the Holy Spirit is a further act by one's spirit in which one invites the full authority of the Holy Spirit to be made manifest in him or her. This requires an awareness of the significance of the experience and a different, deeper brokenness of one's pride. It is the granting of permission for the Holy Spirit to do His will.

Millions of people have had this experience over the last century. If there had not been, perhaps those who reject it as a valid experience for today might be correct. The problem is that those without the experience want to believe that there is no experience to be had. They argue that the experience others have enjoyed is not real. However, in case they are wrong, they have a fall-back position—that they have already received the baptism with the Holy Spirit when they were baptized in water—and they will adamantly argue that they have received it. Because their spirit is often prideful, they cannot and will not admit they may be wrong. Unfortunately, they will go through the remainder of their life deprived of an important step in their Christian walk.

In order to support their view, they argue that the Bible does not record the event, except during the first twenty to thirty years after Pentecost.[134] That may be true, but it's beside the point since the Book of Acts ends before Jerusalem was destroyed in A.D. 70. However, the absence of any written record after the early period in Acts can also mean that the event became expected and was normal. It is probable that the experience was such a usual occurrence that nothing was said about it.

Those that believe the experience stopped over 1,900 years ago will usually

---

133 What confuses the issue is that it is clear the Holy Sprit can either move into us at our water baptism or even at the time of being saved, before water baptism takes place. However, this is not the same as being baptized with the Holy Spirit. It is a difference in our level of surrender to the Holy Spirit and the release of faith. Insofar as the manifestation of the gifts is concerned, that is entirely within the Holy Spirit's control. However, the person must work in conjunction with the Holy Spirit. Thus, it sometimes requires boldness on our part the first time because we are uncomfortable in a new situation. (Note, however, you cannot treat the manifestation of gifts by a person as divine approval of either the person or the message. God in His mercy may cause a healing even though the vehicle or person being used is not of God.)

134 It should be clear that, in most cases, if you do not believe in the experience, it would not occur. Those who reject this experience are unaware that they are being legalistic and that their position is based upon a faulty assumption about the nature of the experience. Often, those with a legalistic approach to their understanding of the Bible ignore every experience accept conversion.

not accept anyone else's current testimony about their experience.[135] This rejection is the work of a legalist spirit. It is a type of religious spirit that convinces a person that God's approval depends on their study and ability to use the Bible as a sword.[136] This attitude has the effect of restricting the manifestation and revelation of the Holy Spirit. This attitude is often associated with an excessive amount of pride concerning their understanding of the Bible. It mainly involves those who believe that the only way to interpret the Bible is with their intellect and by ignoring or excluding anything the Holy Spirit may have to say.[137] They will also believe that the Bible completely contains all that God has to say about everything. Thus, they do not have to deal with weightier issues. They are New Testament Pharisees, using the New Testament as Law.

What is odd about their view on the completeness of the Bible and the pride generated by their belief in their capacity to understand spiritual things, is their failure to recognize that Jesus probably talked about many things that were not included in the Gospels that the Holy Spirit can reveal. It is clear that the Bible is the crucial framework of our faith, which relies upon the Holy Spirit to fill out the structure. This He did, after a manner, with Paul and the other New Testament writers.[138] However, the Holy Spirit did not limit Himself. Although Paul did not specifically write about baptisms, which would have included the

---

135 The gifts of the Holy Spirit were being manifested in approximately A.D. 150. During that time, Justin Martyr wrote that Christians were casting out spirits and healing people, while non-Christians were trying exorcism and using drugs on the sick. This would have been well after the last apostle died and Revelation was written. Thus, if they were being manifest over one hundred years after Jesus died, why not still now?

136 Jesus encouraged study of the Scriptures (John 5:39). Paul, in 2 Timothy 3:16 wrote that Scripture is useful for teaching, rebuking, correcting and training in righteousness. However, our mental accomplishment concerning Scripture is more for our pride and sense of self-worth. The Scriptures, when used in love, as Paul indicated, and not as a weapon to destroy people, can be used to destroy the works of Satan.

137 These are Christians who have a measure of the Holy Spirit within them. It is not, however, the same as being baptized with the Holy Spirit.

138 Recognize that God will not entrust His plans for the world upon any one human, obviously excluding Jesus. In addition, plans go through phases. Thus, everything God had planned for the church was not necessarily revealed in the first century. Christian denominations should remain open for new movements of the Holy Spirit. They must be tested, however, because Satan has not given up yet.

baptism with the Holy Spirit, it certainly is no justification to believe that the experience ceased during the early Christian church period (Heb. 6:2).[139]

Clearly, there is no reason to assume that God has withdrawn any of the gifts of the Holy Spirit until Jesus returns, particularly since the church has not been fully established. There is no reason to believe manifestations of the gifts are not available today merely because they are not widely written about in the United States. Clearly, even though it is sometimes difficult, everyone should be open to the Holy Spirit and submitted to His direction.

HAS ANYTHING CHANGED SINCE THE EARLY CHURCH?

There were times during the Old Testament period and even during Jesus' time on Earth when the Holy Spirit anointed people. However, on the day of Pentecost, fifty days after the Jewish Passover, at which time Jesus was crucified, a new experience was encountered in which the Holy Spirit anointed large groups of believers in Christ.[140] Some of these events were described in Acts. As previously indicated, although this baptism is still available today, some do not recognize it as a separate event from the salvation experience and water baptism.

As indicated previously, the baptism with the Holy Spirit is still a valid experience for today. Contrary to those that reject the concept, it was not just valid for the first one hundred years as a means to create or establish the Christian church. Those who deny that it is a separate event argue that they received it when they were baptized with water, because the speaker invoked the name of the Holy Spirit as part of the ritual. This argument is made even if they do not believe it is something that is a real experience.[141] Others will just argue that the event passed away when the church was established.

It is unclear what the criteria are that such individuals use to define the time

---

139 The generally accepted view is that Paul wrote Hebrews, but scholars believe it may have been Barnabas or Apollo, although most evidence tends to support Paul as the author. Perhaps written between A.D. 64 and 67, this would have been over thirty years after Pentecost.

140 Pentecost was the Jewish Feast of Weeks (Tobit 2:1).

141 One can receive salvation and still have some pride, but to receive the baptism with the Holy Spirit is a different, more humbling experience.

when the church was established.[142] Christianity still had not been fully established as the predominate religion in the world. In fact, most of the religions in the world are rooted in the spirit of Antichrist. For that matter, the Book of Revelation indicates that Christianity will not be a universally accepted truth even at the end of time. If full establishment is not the criteria, than it is merely a matter of opinion of when the church was or will be established. Thus, baptism with the Holy Spirit is still available because the church has not been fully established. Besides, it is a blessing from God. Jesus did not say it was only for a season with limited application.

The Book of Acts, written by Luke when he joined Paul in his travels, records some of the events concerning the baptism with the Holy Spirit.[143] A group of men had been baptized for repentance of sin, but they had not heard of Jesus and they were then baptized into the name of Jesus (Acts 19:2–6). Paul laid hands on them, and they received the baptism with the Holy Spirit and not only spoke with tongues but also prophesied.

The exact steps, timing, and time span involved is undisclosed by Luke. There are, however, several important facts recorded by Luke. There were about twelve men involved, and they were not Christians. First, they became Christians by acceptance of Jesus. They were baptized in water in the name of Jesus. Second, Paul took an additional step, namely, laying hands upon them.[144] Luke did not record what Paul prayed. More than likely, he prayed for the baptism with the Holy Spirit. Third, they demonstrated, without being coached, the power of the

---

142 It is unknown whether they are arguing that the church was established after the first Gospel was written or after the books in the New Testament were agreed upon or some other significant event. Some Christians believe that certain gifts of the Holy Spirit, namely tongues, healing, and prophecy, ceased after the last book of the Bible was written. Others believe it was when the last apostle died. Yet, healings by God still occur today, and God is still with us. Therefore, one should ask why it is not a valid experience since the Bible does not say it will cease before Jesus returns. Any doubts should favor a blessing like this to continue until Jesus returns.

143 Luke also recorded that Jesus said that the Father would give the Holy Spirit to those who ask for it (Luke 11:13). Later, in Luke 24:49, Jesus reminded the apostles that He would send what the Father had promised. In addition, that they would be clothed in power. In other words, they would receive the baptism with the Holy Spirit.

144 Luke does not give any indication of the lapse of time between verses 5 and 6. Those who take the view that the baptism with the Holy Spirit ceased before Acts was completely written assume that there was no meaningful time lapse and that the Holy Spirit was imparted at the time of water baptism. Thus, they believe that if the name of the Trinity was invoked, the baptism was automatic. This ignores many factors. What happens if the speaker does not invoke the Holy Spirit? Is the power and action of the Holy Sprit limited by the person who invokes the blessing? Or, is it more dependent on the recipient's spirit and his desire for the experience?

Holy Spirit when He was manifesting Himself through them.[145] However, was this a single event or two, related events close in time? One should not put too much of a legalistic analysis on Luke's description to the point that it becomes a doctrine limiting what the Holy Spirit might do in this era of faith.

Today, not everyone will immediately manifest one of the visible evidences referenced in Acts at the time of the baptism with the Holy Spirit.[146] However, it is clear that you have to know that the experience is available, and you have to desire it for yourself.[147] Yu must have the right spirit. A proud, guarded, or unbelieving heart will not open the door for the experience. Further, the experience will not occur against your will, so you must desire it.

Paul directly makes no mention of the baptism with the Holy Spirit, although he does talk about the gifts and power of the Holy Spirit. However, we probably do not have copies of all of his letters. He may have written some during the first ten years of his ministry. It is important, however, to recognize that he was usually writing to established churches as opposed to new churches. This could have been one of the reasons why Paul did not mention it. He did not see the need. Remember, he thought that teachings about the different baptisms were elementary (Heb. 6:1–2).

The baptism with the Holy Spirit is also a vital step that hastens the process of sanctification, a process that can also could be called the baptism with fire, which John the Baptist spoke of concerning Jesus (Matt. 3:11; Luke 3:16).[148] This terminology is not mentioned again in the Bible.

It must be pointed out that there is much confusion regarding the gifts of the Holy Spirit. However, speaking a prayer language is not one of the listed gifts described as selectively distributed by the Holy Spirit. Thus, it is available to all, but it is not a requirement as evidence of having experienced the baptism with the Holy Spirit. In other words, you can be baptized with the

---

145 There is no uniformity in how the Holy Spirit will manifest Himself. That depends on the individual. He will not make the person do things not within that person's character. Speaking in tongues is great, but it is not the deciding evidence of the baptism with the Holy Spirit.

146 Some Pentecostal groups believe the only evidence of the baptism is when it is accompanied by speaking in tongues. This is merely being legalistic. The Holy Spirit is not bound by those rules.

147 It is not an automatic thing. You can be saved, called into the ministry, and even receive an anointing for preaching, and you may still not have the baptism with the Holy Spirit. This is particularly true if your background or religious training has convinced you that the gifts are not manifested today because they are unnecessary.

148 Fire often means a refining process, like burning way dross. Some argue that the fire John speaks of means hell. However, because John did not say "with the Holy Spirit or with fire," it is unlikely that the terms were meant to be opposites.

Holy Spirit but not have moved into that dimension of prayer.[149] That experience is also hindered by a lack of knowledge or pride. Once you have moved into that arena, it is easily recognized as a blessing from God.

Some believe that there must be some outward manifestation of the baptism with the Holy Spirit or else it is not a genuine experience. However, a religious spirit can also manifest fake tongues. Therefore, manifestations made in public can be deceiving to onlookers and may be for their approval. It should not be difficult to conclude that the Holy Spirit can do what He wills in conjunction with the person's spirit. He is not one to shove something onto a person until that person desires and wants it. By far one of the most beneficial blessings for us is the release of a prayer language we can pray with in the spirit so that no one else except God can hear and understand.[150] That blesses us, particularly if the Holy Spirit brings to our mind the interpretation of what our spirit has communicated to God. Being able to speak a foreign language may bless someone else who does not speak your native language. However, it is more of a witness to them (1 Cor. 14:22).

Reasons for the Baptism with the Holy Spirit

- It brings you under command of the Holy Spirit for all aspects of your life.
- It gives a new level of authority against Satan and his evil spirits.
- It opens the door for a new and different level of communication with God, as well as a new level of worship.
- It opens the door to receive new levels of wisdom and understanding within the Bible.
- Those with the baptism are less likely to be deceived by Satan.
- The baptism matures and expands the kingdom of God within us.

---

149 The tongue is the hardest part of your flesh to control (James 3:5–6), and it reveals your heart (Matt. 12:34). However, once you have released your tongue to the Holy Spirit, it becomes the avenue to quickly bypass the flesh mind.

150 Usually when Paul used the word *tongues*, he was referring to situations where the expression was heard by others and someone else interpreted the tongue, or message, into a language that others could understand. While he did not use the term *prayer language* in the Scriptures, he did refer to praying to God in a tongue by the Holy Spirit through your spirit (1 Cor. 14:14–17; Rom. 8:26). Your prayer language is not meant for others to hear, for it lifts your spirit in agreement with the Holy Spirit. However, if you feel led to speak out loud for others to hear, the message should be interpreted, by the speaker or by someone else.

How Do You Receive the Baptism?

- You must desire, hunger and thirst, for the baptism.
- By faith, in your heart, receive the promise.[151]
- You cannot have a proud spirit.

How Do You Move in the Holy Spirit?

- Let your actions be motivated by love, but recognize they may still be immature.
- Do not seek to fulfill the pride of the flesh.
- Be ready to change if prompted by the Holy Spirit.
- Sanctify your life. This is not becoming religious![152] Instead, it involves a purifying of your spirit such that you can pray in truth and by the spirit (John 4:23–24).

Summary of Major Points

Two groups of Christians have difficulty with the baptism with the Holy Spirit. The first believes that the experience ended centuries ago. The second group believes it is something that automatically occurs during water baptism if you are baptized in the name of the Holy Spirit. Both of these positions need reevaluation.

The Holy Spirit will not force the experience of baptism on you to ensure that you have the opportunity to learn of the experience. In the beginning, the apostles did not know about the experience before the first time it happened, as recorded in Acts 2. Later on, those who had gone through the experience told others of the opportunity.

You must desire the experience. It will not come to a proud spirit.

More than likely, you will not encounter the same signs that occurred in Acts.

The experience increases the likelihood that you will be able to be used by the Holy Spirit. However, the absence of manifestations of any of the gifts of the Holy Spirit is not necessarily a reflection on you. The timing and

---

151 Being in a church service can help your faith.

152 It is critical that a religious spirit be resisted and cast out. It is just as likely to also be in those without the baptism, but it may express itself differently depending on the level of permissible actions within a person's place of worship.

expression of the baptism is dependent on the Holy Spirit. It is not a measure of your worthiness.

It is a critical step to help hasten the sanctification and maturing process. Its absence will hinder this process.

7

SANCTIFICATION AND MATURING

What Is the Sanctification Process?

ONSIDER JESUS' WORDS to His disciples: "If anyone desires to come after Me, let him deny himself, and take up his cross, and follow Me. For whoever desires to save his life will lose it, but whoever loses his life for My sake will find it" (Matt. 16:24–25, NKJV). Was Jesus speaking of more than salvation? Does the cross we take up represent the death of self—the sanctification process—as we become conformed to the image of Christ (Rom. 8:29)?

In 2 Thessalonians 2:13, Paul wrote, "But we ought always to thank God for you, brothers loved by the Lord, because from the beginning God chose you to be saved through the sanctifying work of the Spirit and through belief in the truth." Peter also wrote about "the sanctifying work of the Spirit" (1 Pet.1:2). Furthermore, early Christians often referred to the Holy Spirit as the Sanctifier.

What did Paul and Peter mean by the term *sanctification*? In simple terms, this means to purify our spirit. It is a process that begins after salvation but intensifies after the baptism with the Holy Spirit. This purification causes us to become closer to Jesus and to mature. One of the consequences is that it produces more love and greater faith. This process renews our mind, it brings our thoughts into captivity, our emotions are brought under control, and our will is conformed to the will of God, as revealed by the Holy Spirit and Jesus.[153] It continues and could be called the baptism with fire spoken of by John the Baptist.

Thus, in order to fellowship with God more closely, we need to ask God to destroy the works of Satan within us. This usually means sin, as well as some of the "personality" traits we have from Satan, such as being bitter, mean-spirited,

---

153 In essence, it is an overcoming life that involves (1) a crucifixion of yourself (your attitudes, fleshly habits); (2) a resurrection (a new life, attitudes, etc.); and (3) an ascension (in a spiritual manner).

proud, arrogant, fearful, depressed, resentful, feeling rejected or unworthy, angry, hateful, unloving, envious, and jealous, to name a few. Some of these traits are merely flesh, but if they cannot be overcome after diligent prayer and taking them to Jesus, perhaps an evil spirit has been given tacit permission to reside within us.

During the process of change, we can mistakenly believe that God is testing us and causing trials to occur. Satan is doing the testing, if in fact any is done at all.[154] Satan has the right to challenge us, as illustrated in the Book of Job. God loves us, but Satan has been given the right to prove his case that his ejection from heaven, with an eventual destination in hell, is not justified.

One way of closing the door to Satan is to deal with our lusts and any other negative attributes. We close that door by asking Jesus to point out those areas that need changing so that we can ask Him to remove the hindrance.[155] The process, however, does not happen until we are ready to let go of the weakness that needs to be changed. Some are easier to change than others are. While we will never be perfect, we should desire to remove anything that hinders our relationship with Jesus and our ability to pray in truth. (For those issues that cannot be changed with prayer alone, one should suspect that a spirit may be associated with the behavior and the motivation behind it. In that case, it would need to be dealt with through spiritual warfare and deliverance ministry.) Keep in mind that every Christian enters into the kingdom of God violently by pressing through desire, by the exercising of our will, and when necessary, with tribulation (Luke 16:16).

What are the biggest obstacles to becoming a mature Christian who is able to distinguish good from evil (Heb. 5:14)? There are three: the lust of the eyes, the lust of the flesh, and the pride of life. These three major obstacles contain several parts or sub-issues that affect all of us. Throughout the process of change or purification, the Holy Spirit is a guide, a teacher, and sometimes but rarely a disciplinarian in the life of a Spirit-filled person.

How is Satan going to attack the changes that are taking place in the Christian as he or she is sanctified? Satan will first attempt to attack your weaknesses.

---

154 One could argue that God indirectly allows Satan to test us. With that reasoning, however, every bad thing that life brings could be attributed to God. Yes, God created life. Nevertheless, as expected by God, man changed the dynamics of what we call life. It now has bad times, but God is not to blame. Satan became an integral part of our life. However, God has placed limitations upon him. In any event, God never tempts us with evil. He doesn't promote sin or desire us to sin.

155 Generally, in this process, God will use circumstances to cause us to recognize the area that needs to be changed. However, it can be a long process, and if we are not careful, we can become insensitive.

Satan can easily attack our mind. He can create feelings of guilt, discouragement, rejection, and despair. These negative thoughts and emotions attack our spirit with a feeling of unworthiness, even though we have become worthy in God's eyes because of Jesus. In order to fight Satan and his attacks more successfully, it is critical that you experience the baptism with the Holy Spirit. Without the baptism with the Holy Spirit, the sanctification process can still occur, but it is limited because you have guarded your spirit rather than relinquishing control to the Holy Spirit.

It is clear that the kingdom of God does not consist of meat and drink. It is "righteousness, peace and joy in the Holy Spirit" (Rom. 14:17). This is not something that comes upon you without your participation. It is not a passive activity. Instead, it requires an effort on your part, an effort spent to change your inner man. In all of this, Jesus is the author and perfector of the changes, which produces greater love of Him and an increased level of faith (Heb. 12:2). Our level of faith is directly proportional to our love of Jesus above all else.

While Jesus changes us, Satan wars against us in our physical body through illness and pain; in our soul through our feelings such as anxiety, fear, and guilt; and in our spirit by attacking our confidence and faith in Jesus. The real war is spiritual in nature. The Holy Spirit will draw our attention to the problem areas. It is a process of obtaining holiness. However, we have to be open and sensitive to the Spirit. In rare situations, deliverance may be necessary.

QUESTIONS WE NEED TO ASK OURSELVES AS WE GO THROUGH THE SANCTIFICATION PROCESS

- Is what motivates us true to the character of God?
- Does this activity violate God's plans?[156]
- Is the result of our activity an extension of the life and works of Jesus?
- Does this activity violate the principles in the New Testament?

Sadly, Christians can be in bondage to the New Testament when it is interpreted by the intellect and in a manner similar to the Jews and the Old Testament, that is, with the creation of rules and laws. Man likes to have rules to follow, even when he fails to follow them. Rules establish the parameter of the permissible

---

156 For example, homosexuality violates God's plan for procreation and breaks the bond that can develop between man and woman. This bond actually enhances our ability to love and trust God because it is a foretaste of the spiritual bond you will have with the Father.

behavior a person believes God will find acceptable. Undefined areas or principles of behavior, established by faith, are more difficult to manage because
pride, as measured by our compliance, deludes us about our true state or progress. Thus, rules control our flesh; they don't change our heart.

Salvation causes a renewed spirit within us, but the baptism with the Holy
Spirit accelerates the process of changing our spirit, such that the New Testament becomes a living Word that is revealed by the Holy Spirit. The living
Word changes us as we obtain purity, wisdom, understanding, and maturity. In
effect, the Holy Spirit begins to conform or change our spirit into the likeness
of Jesus. Throughout this process of change, one undergoes the pain of change.
You suffer with Christ by letting the maturing spirit rule over your flesh.

WHAT DOES MATURING MEAN?

The writer of Hebrews said that the elementary teachings of the written Word
were like milk for infants (Heb. 5:11–14). He explained that the goal is to train
yourself up to distinguish good from evil. He was not talking about the simple
evil that is obvious to everyone but rather about the distinction between what is
of God and what is merely the good works of man. Thus, the maturing process
enables us to discern the motives and spirit behind people's actions. Even Satan
can appear as an angel of light (2 Cor. 11:14). Thus, not everything that looks
good on the surface is, in fact, of God.

Hebrews 6:1–2 defines what constitute elementary teachings: teachings about
sin and acts that lead to death; repentance and faith in God; as well as doctrines
concerning instructions about baptisms, the laying on of hands, resurrection of
the dead, and eternal judgment.

LEVELS OF SPIRITUAL MATURITY

- Babes in Christ—still carnal (1 Cor. 3:1; 1 Pet. 2:2)
- Children in Christ—tossed to and fro by doctrine (Eph. 4:14)
- Full age—can discern good and evil, pressing to become more
  like Jesus (Heb. 5:13–14)

BENEFITS FROM MATURING

You should determine to mature in Christ, not escape life. The bad times are
events of life that can mature us. They are not trials, tests, or punishment for
God's children.

- We become doers of the Word, not merely hearers. We love without being religious.
- Our spirit becomes changed by the Holy Spirit, not from an observation of laws or rules.
- We become bonded with fellow Christians. They may be different because of differences in understanding and revelation, but they are not our real enemy.[157]
- We may discern and distinguish evil spirits from emotions.
- We develop the ability to understand the difference between flesh activities and spiritual activities, both within yourself and within others.[158]

PROGRESS OF MATURITY

Event	Purpose	Result
Salvation (repentance of sins)	Spirit reborn (one is a babe in Christ)	Witness of Christ by our testimony
Baptism with the Holy Spirit	Testimony by the fruit of our spirit	We are more available to be used by the Holy Spirit
Baptism with fire	(1)Beginning of purification of our spirit, (2) increase of faith, (3) greater tendency to lean toward holiness rather than sin, (4) increased ability to be led by the Spirit	We are more likely to be used by the Holy Spirit and more likely to receive insight and wisdom from God

---

157 Not every claimed Christian denomination is Christian. The key differences appear to be whether they believe that Jesus (the Word) existed as part of God before the Incarnation; that He came, lived a life subject to temptation, died sinless as the eternal sacrifice for our sin, and was resurrected and sits with God, the Father; that salvation is only through Jesus; and that our good deeds will not bring salvation.

158 Modern churches fail to understand that what is often called worship is nothing more than flesh seeking attention. This is particularly represented in music. Music is sometimes called worship when in fact it does not even reach the level of praise. It is merely religious flesh.

Event	Purpose	Result
Lifelong sanctification process (we will never become perfect)	(1) a maturing spirit, (2) know the character of God, (3) respond to His will, (4) flesh becomes more controlled, (5) wisdom and knowledge increase, (6) increased ability to be led by the Spirit	Through a more intimate level of faith we may walk with God, have dominion over our body, and will be better able to defeat Satan and pray in truth and by the Spirit.

WHAT IS CONFUSED AS MATURITY?

- It is not acquired by separating yourself from the world.
- It is not dependent on the amount of time spent in prayer and fasting.
- It clearly is not dependent on obedience to rules and laws of the church.[159]
- It does not depend on attendance or support for a church. However, the church is a support structure that should be part of your life. Being part of a church does facilitate the release of the Spirit of God within you.
- It does not use extreme emotions when worshiping God. (These are just religious spirits at work. They like to draw attention to themselves in an effort to justify themselves to God.)

So what is the maturing experience? It occurs through a number of activities, not just one. The most important is spending time with Jesus, not only when praying but at various other times. It will also occur through worship, prayer, and reading the Bible and meditating on it (placing it in your heart). These are not to be done out of compulsion but because He is the most important part of your life and you desire to express your love of Him. It is also done with balance, having the assurance that He is always there for you. You may fast in order to bring your appetites and flesh under your authority. Later on, as you begin to mature, you will notice how you begin to understand yourself. This is not to say that you will be perfect, but over what is sometimes a long period of time, some deeply entrenched aspects of who you really are begin to

---

159 This is not to mean we are rebellious.

change—for the better. Don't, however, expect to completely change immediately. God still loves you, and He will show you what needs to change.

Some churches have more freedom for you to express yourself in worship. These are great, but what is important is the relationship you and Jesus have when you are alone. While you need the freedom to express your worship, God does not desire disorder, because it draws attention to yourself. It can also harm new Christians. Thus, be considerate and allow your love and maturity to be reflected in your worship.

Ask for the Holy Spirit to give you understanding that the process of maturation is not intellectual but an understanding that flows from your heart. Recognize that it is tied together with the sanctification process. The Bible cannot be truly understood by our intellect, but only by the Spirit of God (1 Cor. 2:7–14). It must be spiritually discerned. The intellect will see illustrations and make doctrines out of them (Luke 8:10–11).[160] Often this is done as an ego exercise to lift oneself up in the eyes of man. Although they will not admit it, they seek to receive the glory and praise of their contemporaries.

WISDOM

Wisdom, which God gives to us, is a valuable tool (Col. 1:9; James 1:5). Paul stated in 1 Corinthians 1:30, "It is because of Him [God] that you are in Christ Jesus, who has become for us wisdom from God—that is, our righteousness, holiness, and redemption." Thus, Jesus is the basis of our wisdom. Paul also said in Ephesians 1:17, "I keep asking that the God of our Lord Jesus Christ, the glorious Father, may give you the Spirit of wisdom and revelation, so that you may know Him better." However, what is it? It is not merely a single concept, approach, or experience, but a combination of these, as well as insight and revelation from God. A starting point for wisdom is to extrapolate an idea or concept into a wider application.

For example, consider prayer and healing. If God healed everyone who prayed for healing, then we would be able to conclude that if a person was sick, the person had not prayed. If there were conditions under which a prayer must be performed, such as a "right" spirit, then if the individual were sick, it would mean they did not have a right spirit. In other words, any condition, unsatisfied, would prevent the healing from occurring. In effect, we would exist under a cause-and-effect relationship. In other words, we would be under a system of

---

160 For example, many other denomination-specific doctrines are based upon man's attempt to understand "mysteries" in the Bible, which only the Holy Spirit can explain.

laws and rules instead of an era of faith. This system was what existed at the time Jesus came and what He replaced.

Recall that in Jesus' day, people judged the righteousness of a person by their illness. Sin was understood to be the reason for sickness, illness, or any misfortune of life. One's health and happiness were dependent on how well he or she was trained by their parents, society, and the religious establishment. Perhaps this explains why most religions today, except Christianity, still exist under that concept of cause and effect, reward and punishment. Thus, they have a total misunderstanding of God and the purposes of God.

Again, if homosexuality were acceptable, then everyone should be able to exercise that option. In addition, if they did, it would not be very long before humanity would cease to exist on Earth. Clearly, God's plans and purposes would be blocked. Sometimes elementary wisdom is merely carrying an idea to its conclusion. At other times it involves the need to understand the basic underlying principles. Like, what is man's purpose? If that is understood, other concepts can be built upon it.

The primary source of wisdom is from God. With His Spirit within us, we can begin to see things or evaluate situations from His perspective of truth. Pray, therefore, for His wisdom.

SUMMARY OF MAJOR POINTS

- Sanctification is a process in which our spirit is brought into the likeness of Jesus by the power of the Holy Spirit.
- Negative emotions and/or spirits need to be expunged from our spirit.
- Sanctification is a lifelong process through the Holy Spirit, but the Lord gives wisdom every step of the way.
- Maturing in the Spirit is an experience in which we become able to discern good from evil. We become better able at recognizing the true motives behind people's words and actions. We also are better able to discern the motives behind our own words and actions.
- Our relationship with God becomes more intimate. Our love for Him increases, and our faith increases.

8

MISCONCEPTIONS ABOUT CHRISTIANITY

ARE YOU DRIVEN BY GOD?

YOU SHOULD NEVER be driven by anything. God does not drive or force you to do anything. He stands at the door and knocks. Satan, on the other hand, will do everything he can to drive you to act a certain way. Guilt, anger, resentment, fear, rejection, greed, and negative emotions can open the door for spirits to enter us.[161] When that occurs, then you will be driven by these feelings. They will control you and even shape how other people see you. They can be overcome with the direct help of the Holy Spirit.

Perhaps the classic case of how Satan can deceive a person, indicated in the New Testament, is the case of Judas Iscariot. Luke wrote that Satan entered Judas. John said Judas had been prompted by Satan and that Satan entered him during the Last Supper before he went to betray Jesus. (See John 13:27, NKJV.) Jesus, however, knew from the beginning, before time began, that Judas would betray Him (Matt. 26:2; Mark 10:33; Luke 18:32). Still, He chose him to be a disciple. Whatever Judas' reasons for betrayal, they were not a sudden or uncontrolled plan on his part. He had his own agenda that he thought would force Jesus to take certain actions. Even though Judas was under Jesus' ministry for so long, he still had his own agenda, which went counter to all Jesus said about His purposes, including His death, illustrates an obsessed and driven person. Obsession is also one of the indicators of a driven person. Satan, not God, drives a person. Satan will use evil spirits to make people feel compelled to act a certain way, particularly for religious purposes.[162]

Paul said we should be led by the Spirit (Rom. 8:14; Gal. 5:18). When we are

---

161 It takes a persistent period in which an individual surrenders to a specific negative emotion before an evil spirit might gain access to your spirit. It is something that does occur automatically.

162 Unfortunately, some Christian leaders have religious spirits within them that drive not only themselves but also the church members. These individuals often believe that God has called them to "protect" the faith.

83

led by the Spirit we are no longer under the Law or the compulsion that the Law creates (2 Cor. 9:7), nor are we in bondage to Satan's way of tempting us to act.

DOES GOD TEST PEOPLE?

In 2 Corinthians 13:5, Paul said to test ourselves to see if Jesus is in us. In other letters, he said we should test ourselves, particularly our actions, and everything else (Gal. 6:4). When you have performed the text, "hold on to the good" (1 Thess. 5:21). John says to test the spirits, meaning, discern what spirits are at work in people (1 John 4:1). (It is of worth to note that there is a spiritual gift called the discerning of spirits. (See 1 Corinthians 12:10.) James says that persecution for Christ's sake is a test (James 1:12), and the writer of Hebrews encouraged followers to distinguish or discern good from evil (5:12).

In spite of all these verses, there do not appear to be any references in the New Testament in which God tests us. (I am not talking about the challenges that one faces through the process of sanctification.) God does not test people unless Jesus is not in them.[163]

It is clear that when we first move into new areas of the Holy Spirit's leading, it will usually be a challenge just because it is something new, but this is not a test. Instead, it is a challenge to our old self. The idea is to learn something new. When you teach a child to ride a bike, is it a test or is it a part of being trained for a new experience? The child may test themselves with new experiences so they can develop confidence for even more new and difficult experiences. We, as parents, may even create opportunities for growth. However, we are not testing them unless we threaten the withdrawal of our love if they fail to measure up to our expectations. Our love is not given as a reward. Neither is God's love. Thus, approval from God is not dependent on passing a series of tests. As His children, He loves us more then we love ourselves.

It is life and Satan that test people. God, of course, does not always prevent adverse things from occurring to us. He allows some because that is part of life, a byproduct of sin. However, we have the assurance that regardless of the adversity, we will come through it. The issue is what you do under those situations and if you allow them to challenge your love for God.

---

163 Paul said in 2 Corinthians 13:5 to test yourself. John said to test the spirits (1 John 4:1). Jesus said He would test the whole world, except the saints (Rev. 3:10). To be sure, one's work will be tested. (See 1 Corinthians 3:13; James 1:13.)

TEMPTATION

Our first instinct is to avoid temptation. In some religions, those people who tempt others are punished. In many cases, established norms of behavior are tailored toward the prevention of temptation. The classical example is the standard of clothing worn by females. If the clothing a woman wears is outside of the prescribed norms, she is punished.

Temptation, however, actually molds us. It brings to the surface feelings, beliefs, and reactions that need to be addressed and should be treated as an opportunity for spiritual growth. This is part of the sanctification process. Eventually, we will overcome as we mature. Thus, like Jesus, we should not run away or create controls to prevent temptations.[164]

It is not an easy thing to deal with temptations. Everyone fails at some point, if not initially. That is why they are temptations. First, one needs to prevent the failures from searing our conscience. In other words, do not give up changing until that particular set of circumstances is no longer a temptation. People are exposed to many temptations. However, God will not allow you to be put into a situation you are unable to handle. In addition, He will provide a way out (1 Cor. 10:13).

Greed is among the most common temptations in our nation (1 Tim. 6:9). Suppose, for example, we believe we may be allowing greed to influence our decisions. How do we handle the temptation? One way is to avoid temptation by not allowing ourselves to be placed in situations where we might be tempted. Unfortunately, though, this limits our ability to interact with society. The second way is to treat the situation as a challenge to grow from or to change because of it.

By challenging ourselves, we deliberately recognize that temptation may occur but that with the help of Jesus, we will be given strength to recognize it and overcome it. In the process, we will come to realize that there are no fixed rules or standards that you can impose upon yourself to control your choices.

---

164 Most controls involve a method of hindering the commitment of sin. However, the condition of our spirit either allows or prevents sin at their source. After you are saved, your spirit becomes more sensitive to situations that cause you to sin. In time, you will develop an immunity to particular situations that tempted you to sin in the past. Successes cause your spirit to reject the temptation so that eventually you don't even have to weigh or consider situations; you automatically reject the temptation. The classic example of a poor spiritual condition allowing sin is that of rejection. It will motivate us to say and do things to avoid rejection, regardless of the harm to others. The desire to gain acceptance will overcome all warnings from the Holy Spirit because the need for acceptance is first in your life.

Instead, there are two things you must recognize: first, that you are potentially subject to temptation, but you will not attempt to avoid it;[165] second, that because of Jesus you will have strength to overcome whatever the temptation and grow from the experience. Eventually you will be immune to the temptation.

IS THERE A PLACE FOR ANGER?

Righteous anger can release faith. However, it must be anger from the spirit, not your flesh.

What made Jesus angry?

- The abuse of people in the house of God.
- People who blasphemed the Holy Spirit.
- Religious leaders that placed heavy burdens on people, particularly religious burdens.
- Widows being taken advantage of, especially by religious people.
- Those that neglect justice, mercy, compassion and faith but exalt legalism (Mark 3:1–5).
- Evil spirits at work.

Jesus, at times, became frustrated. For example, several times He commented on the lack of faith of His disciples (Matt. 16:8; 17:17). Paul said, "'In your anger do not sin:' Do not let the sun go down while you are still angry, and do not give the devil a foothold" (Eph. 4:26–27). James said, "Everyone should be quick to listen, slow to speak and slow to become angry, for man's anger does not bring about the righteous life that God desires" (James 1:19). Once, Jesus called Herod a fox (Luke 13:32).

Paul recognized that we, in fact, do get angry. However, Paul was concerned by outbursts of anger, as well as the lingering effects of it (2 Cor. 12:20). He said to get rid of it (Col. 3:8; Eph. 4:31). Outbursts of anger, or as James states, sudden anger, can indicate an uncontrolled emotion that occurs in reaction to situations. This problem needs to be dealt with through spiritual warfare.

---

165 The issue of addiction recovery follows a somewhat different path to victory, as intentional avoidance of the addictive substance or substances is often wise. It is crucial to recognize that addictions can have as a root source a "spirit of addiction," which is why some recovering addicts move from one substance to another. Deliverance is necessary to overcome this kind of addiction. The first step is to seek Jesus and commit to changing your desire for the substance or the behavior pattern that causes you to sin. If this is unsuccessful, seek help from a spiritual counselor who can recognize the spirit's domination.

Disappointments, frustrations, and the like are part of life. Outbursts are not a proper response and indicate there could be a spiritual problem, particularly if it becomes physically expressed by attacking people.

Do Material Rewards Resulting from Obedience Await You in Heaven?

Jesus indicated that there would be rewards in heaven (Matt. 5:12; Luke 6:23). Paul wrote in Colossians 3:24, that we would receive an inheritance from Jesus as a reward. The nature of these rewards is not indicated. Some believe Paul was writing about the humble spirit one should have when inheriting the kingdom of heaven. It is certain there will be a righteous man's reward and a prophet's reward (Matt. 10:41). However, what the reward is, other than being with God, is not specifically stated.

Does God Bless You for How You Manage Money?

We are in the Era of Faith, no longer in a reward-punishment era. Jesus actually addressed the issue of financial blessings and money management in an indirect way in the Sermon on the Mount. He said, "Give, and it will be given to you. A good measure, pressed down, shaken together and running over, will be poured into your lap. For with the measure you use, it will be measured to you" (Luke 6:38). Notice He said nothing about obligations established by religious institutions. Notice also, this statement could refer to the giving of your love, compassion, and yourself, not just money.

Is Tithing a Requirement?

Tithing was a concept that appears to have started with Abraham and his one-tenth offering of the spoils of a battle to King Melchizedek of Salem, who was also a priest of God, after he had brought out bread and wine and blessed Abraham (Gen. 14:20).[166] There is no record that the one-tenth offering was anything other than a means of showing gratitude.

---

166 God established a concept of a priest before the establishment of the Law and the Levitical priesthood. Moses, the initial author of the first five books of the Old Testament, did not elaborate on the origin of the priestly position. However, David mentions Melchizedek in Psalm 110:4, and Paul makes extensive references to Melchizedek in Hebrews. By mentioning that the priesthood of Melchizedek predated the Law, Paul was indirectly challenging the concept that the Jewish law was the final and only means of determining righteousness.

The next person recorded to have set aside a one-tenth offering to God was Jacob (Gen. 28:22). After leaving Egypt, the one-tenth concept became part of some of the sin offerings (Exod. 29:40). Eventually man made the concept of giving one-tenth or a tithe a means of atonement. It became a means of offsetting their sin. Later, Jesus pointed out that the religious leaders were addressing acts of the flesh, including tithing, and ignoring weightier spiritual issues (Matt. 23:23).

While Jesus was incarnated on Earth, He was still under the Law. When His actions were challenged, he addressed the more important matters we should be concerned with, such as mercy. Present-day church leaders often quote Jesus as telling the religious leaders that tithing was something they were supposed to do. They were, since they were still under the Law. However, the Law was replaced by this era of faith (Rom. 3:28). Church leaders know this, but they are under the pressure of their budgets. However, many people mistakenly replace faith with tithing, because it is a rule that can be followed.

After Jesus' resurrection, things changed. You will notice that tithing is not mentioned in Acts or in Paul's letters. Instead, Paul wants us to be sensitive to the Holy Spirit and follow His leading. (See Romans 8:14; Galatians 5:18, NKJV.) Paul said for special offerings (not the normal offering), to set aside and save up, proportional to one's income (1 Cor. 16:2).

Tithing, however, is a guide, particularly for a new Christian.[167] As a member of a church, one has an obligation to support that church in a fair manner. This is related to your income, but there is no prescribed percentage. If you are unable to hear specifically from the Holy Spirit, until you are able, your contribution to support the church should be based upon principles of fairness as it relates to many factors, including your income. It will involve your discipline, dedication, and love of the Lord, in that you are supporting the Lord's work on Earth. However, if your giving takes away from your ability support your family's needs, then it is too much and may be either a source of pride or a self-righteous act. Both of these are to be avoided.[168]

Unfortunately, when the church falls back into or adopts an Old Testament principle such as tithing to institute it as a rule, it is detrimental to members. Rather than helping the members to mature spiritually so they can be led by

---

167 If every Christian were mature, they would hear from the Holy Spirit, and the church would be adequately funded at all times. However, since this maturity can take a number of years to achieve, the tithe is a standard.

168 Regardless of what you contribute, it should be considered the first priority for allocating your money. It cannot be an amount you have left over after other expenses, from loose change, etc. It should be a consistent amount, and your expenses should not erode that commitment.

the Spirit, they are led to believe that tithing is required. Some churches even use the statement that God will bless you thirty, sixty, or one hundred-fold if you tithe. The verse often quoted is taken out of context. In that verse, Jesus was speaking about how much the Word is fruitful when sowed on good soil (Matt. 13:8). When Jesus addressed the issue of giving, it was from a perspective of one's heart condition, not a teaching on tithing (Luke 6:38).

When the appeal to the "legal" aspects of tithing do not motivate the congregation, some leaders resort to a statement in Hebrews that you should obey those over you in the Lord (Heb. 13:17). It says obey those over you and submit to their authority.[169] However, you would only submit when the leaders are in fact following the directions of God.[170] If what they said was something that conflicted with the Bible, then they would be false leaders.[171] It is unclear what the writer of Hebrews was dealing with when he made this statement. It could well have been elementary doctrines of Christianity. It is doubtful that the writer was making a blanket statement that no matter what was said, it should be followed, particularly when it conflicted with the Bible. Therefore, if you are subjected to any of these approaches, recognize that sometimes it is difficult to live by faith, even for leaders of the church.

About tithing, Paul said to give what was decided in your heart and not to be under compulsion. However, he also said that you do reap what you sow (2 Cor. 9:6–7). If you decide you want to tithe, it must be your joy and not under duress. However, recognize that it would be better to remain open to the Holy Spirit's leading. If tithing becomes a law, a rule, or an ordinance followed because of pressure from anyone, including yourself, eventually you will regret it and become angry and bitter about it.

---

169 Various versions of the Bible translate this scripture differently: "your leaders"(ISV, NIV, NRSV), "them that have rule over you" (ASV, KJV), "those that have rule over you" (NKJV), "those leading you" (YLT).

170 Christianity is built upon the freedom of choice. The concept of authority or leadership over you must be something you accept. Thus, find a church where you feel able to follow those that lead the church. However, always resolve those situations where you believe the directions are wrong. This means to seek out truth, and if a conflict remains, it should be resolved. If you cannot accept the position of the leader, it is better to leave than remain. There is no presumption that the leader is always right. However, if you repeatedly have conflict in different churches, then perhaps the problem lies within you.

171 Unfortunately, some church leaders have used their position and the trust of the people to take advantage of them. See *The Subtle Power of Spiritual Abuse* by David Johnson and Jeff Van Vonderen (Bethany House Publishers, 1991).

ARE THE ACTS OF OUR LIVES A WORSHIP OF GOD?

We are to worship God by and with our spirit in truth (John 4:23). To believe your actions or behavior will save you puts you in bondage. In particular, it negates what Jesus did for us. When Christians believe that the flesh man's activities are used to judge their righteousness, it is an erroneous mixture of Old and New Testament principles.

Christians are often told that faith without works or deeds is useless (James 2:14–26).[172] James, however, was not writing about works of the flesh or Law. James was writing about our faith being reflected and expressed by our works or deeds (James 2:22). In other words, the works are evidence of our faith.[173] Works, or good deeds, are not a substitute for faith. Paul stated clearly that man is not justified by works, particularly not by works of the Law, but only by faith (Gal. 2:16; 5:6; Rom. 3:28).[174] The point both are making is that good deeds or good works, if done in an effort to follow a religious law, deceive us into thinking we are justified. The source or reason for the works is what is important. If our hearts are not reflecting our Christian faith and our love of Jesus, they are merely dead activities as far as God is concerned. There would be no true witness, merely the outward man doing what he believes is right, sometimes solely for acceptance. It is not a reflection of your spirit. On the other hand, being a Christian without reflecting your love, compassion, and mercy in a material way to others is empty.

WHAT IS FAITH?

It is important to remember that faith is not a feeling. It is not a manipulation of the mind with positive thoughts. It is not merely hope or even an expectation that because a desired outcome will be good, that thing will happen because God is good. A major hindrance to faith is the observation of facts that challenge us or appear insurmountable (Matt. 14:31). The Word of God has to eventually dwell in your spirit so that you will have faith even when circumstances or feelings fail you.

Faith comes from hearing from God (Rom. 10:17, NKJV). In other words, if God tells you something, then you can count on it. Obviously, if God spoke

---

172 It is believed that the author of the book of James is James the Just, elder of the church at Jerusalem, and half-brother to Jesus.

173 He was writing about having compassion and charity for those in need.

174 *Work or deeds of the Law* refers to acts done out of obligations of the Law. *Works of faith* refers to works that flow from your love and faith in Jesus.

audibly to us, it would not require anything from us except to carry out any responsibility we had or any pre-condition stated by God and wait for the thing promised. Faith comes from hearing within our spirit and responding, if necessary. Hearing from God is not easy because He does not speak any differently than our own mind speaks to us. God interjects His words into our mind, and we have to discern the difference. The best way to avoid the potential for mistake is to compare what we think He has spoken to us against the Bible to see if there is any conflict. If what He seemed to say lines up with the Word, it is likely that it was His voice.

Faith is not evoked because you have read a Bible verse that sounds good and appears to be a promise. You cannot assume that promises in the Bible have universal application and that if you claim it or want it, it will be automatic. It is not effective to couch your request as a demand or right based on a statement in the Bible that you believe is a promise from God, nor will "a positive attitude" bring results. There are usually unstated conditions attached to the promises. Therefore, you must seek God's yes or no to your request. Remember, God is not going to make all of life's problems go away. He cannot if we want to be able to exercise our free will. When He does say yes, the answer is usually not immediate.

So where does faith come from? It comes from your relationship with God. It grows out of and is directly dependent on your relationship with Jesus and your love and trust in Him. (This love and trust are related, with trust being created, as well as increasing, because of your love.) Faith matures as your knowledge, understanding, and love of Jesus mature. Wisdom given to you by God causes your spirit to change. As you mature, you begin to discern when you are expressing your hopes and desires in your mind about a situation and when you actually hear from God about the situation.

It is from this "hearing" or knowing in your spirit that faith is released such that the evidence materializes or occurs.[175] The knowing in your spirit is an extension of that which occurs with the baptism with the Holy Spirit in that you move from merely believing in Jesus to knowing Jesus in a deeper experience, by your spirit (Rom. 10:9–10). The knowing within your spirit is the result of the relationship you have with Jesus.

It is worth repeating that an increasing love for Jesus is a requirement for faith to grow. Our growth is directly dependent on the depth of the love we have for Jesus in our spirit. As you are able to pray in truth by the spirit, the

---

175 See 1 Corinthians 2:9–15. The Spirit reveals all things. The Spirit is the author of our spiritual growth, of our love for Jesus, and the faith that flows out of the love of Jesus.

easier it is to hear from God. Before truth can emerge, your spirit must become more like Jesus. This only occurs as your love of self diminishes and is replaced by your love of Jesus. It is unrelated to religious acts. In fact, generally, religious acts prevent or hinder both love and faith from maturing because pride tempts us to make them a substitute.

One problem with religious acts is that they are often merely fleshly acts that lift up our pride. A second problem is that if they are not based from faith, they are sin.[176] The third problem is that no one is justified before God by the Law, because the righteous will live by faith not works (Gal. 3:11). Therefore, true worship is unrelated to religious acts, thought by man to be special. Faith, instead, grows from being alone with Jesus (2 Cor. 2:15). As your character and spirit change because of your relationship, one does not broadcast or brag about everything that is from Jesus. Be discerning about sharing about the blessings you receive. It is best to be led by the Spirit in these matters because you may create obstacles, such as envy and jealousy, in others.

It should be clear that faith should not be expected to be a means of removing all problems in your life. Even great spiritual men such as the apostle Paul or Smith Wigglesworth likely had physical problems. Those "thorns in their flesh" were recognized as being necessary to keep their feet on the ground. (See 2 Corinthians 12:7.) It reminded them that they were merely human beings and dependent on God. It was nothing within themselves that caused miracles and healings. It was God alone.

Life in our flesh will present or cause many situations we would rather avoid. However, it also presents opportunities. They, however, are never tests by God, either directly or indirectly. They are part of the domain granted to Satan so that God's glory in creation will be made manifest.

MISUNDERSTANDING THE WORD *FAITH*

The word *faith* is used to mean different things depending on the context in which it is used. For example, it is used in the following manner:

- *the faith* as a system of religious beliefs; synonym for *Christianity* (Acts 6:7)
- *faith* as a belief and trust in Jesus (Matt. 6:30; Acts 3:16)

---

176 In Romans 14:23, Paul said that "everything that does not come from faith is sin." In fact, our righteousness comes from a living faith (Rom. 1:17; 3:22) Therefore, good acts of the flesh may be sinful because of the wrong motives and purposes. They hide our true spirit from others.

- *faith* as a conviction based upon revelation from God (Heb. 11:1)
- *faith* as belief in what could be (Matt. 8:26; 14:31)

Many times the word *faith* is used in the wrong way as a synonym for *belief.* However, having faith, which can truly only come from your heart or spirit and not your head, is different. The faith that Jesus and Paul were referring to was more like knowing and trusting Jesus. Thus, as said before, you must get to know Jesus, not merely know about Jesus. When you know Jesus, it is life changing. It is a step beyond belief; a relationship is established. Our trust in Him comes with knowing Him as well as loving Him. In addition, loving him produces greater faith.

Initially, you cannot love Him; you merely know about Him. You move into loving Him as He becomes more important in your life and, from there, to knowing Him. The baptism with the Holy Spirit is vital because it first requires a humbling of your pride before you can be dependent on His love. Being dependent on His love allows you to know Him.

Unfortunately, there have been many Christian leaders throughout the centuries who wanted to serve Him, but they only knew information about Him. They did not actually know Him. They might have even believed they loved Him. However, their pride and intellect prevented them from having an intimate relationship with Him. After all, Jesus said that there would be those who would even be able to cast out demons and do miracles in His name, but they would not be allowed into the kingdom of heaven (Matt. 7:21–23). You can be sure that with those kinds of signs and wonders they would have a large following today, perhaps even a large church. However, these outward manifestations of apparent authority from God are no assurance that they are men of God. If these leaders could deceive themselves, how, except by discernment, will you know they are not to be followed? Their words will reveal whether they really know Jesus or not because "out of the overflow of the heart the mouth speaks" (Matt. 12:34). Another indicator is to look for the fruit of the Spirit in his or her life. Often, the most obvious sign will be the manifestation of pride. Your responsibility is to discern their spirit. This becomes easier when you know Jesus, particularly after the baptism with the Holy Spirit.

HOPE

Hope is vastly different from faith. Hope comes from the combination of our desires and the possibilities we believe could occur. For example, we may desire "good" things for a person, such as healing or a new job. Our expectation, however, is dependent on our belief in what possibilities God can create. When these two concepts—desire and possibility—are combined, we develop a hope that God will change the situation for a person.

Notice that this hope is created mostly from desire. It can be very strong, particularly when it concerns oneself or a loved one. Faith, however, is different because of its source. The distinction is whether you are relying on external evidence for your belief or on your spirit. If we believe a certain biblical reference is a promise to us, it is an external source of information that our mind has evaluated; and when combined with desire, it will create hope.

Hope can change to faith, but only if God speaks to our spirit after we have taken our hope to Him in prayer. Then and only then can you have faith. Thus, faith develops within our spirit, and hope is merely a product of our mind. It is important to recognize the difference and to know when God has spoken. This is not an easy task, because one can become obsessed by his or her desire and then fail to hear God, particularly if He says no.

ANSWERS TO PRAYER

Prayer involves the complete yielding of your spirit to the will of Jesus. It is a time of intimate closeness in which you believe that He knows your every need and you request His mercy and intervention. It is never your right to demand or to believe that God is obligated to intervene. When we feel that way, our prayers leave our spirit empty; the problem lies within us. Do not give up until you know His will in your spirit, whatever that may be, so that your prayers can be in line with His purposes and plan.

In this era of faith, one of the pitfalls we fall into is thinking that whenever we are not healed or bad times are not prevented, it was because of a lack of faith on our part. The problem is the misunderstanding of what faith really is. Faith, as described in the Book of Hebrews, is not easy to understand.

> Now faith is being sure of what we hope for, and certain of what we do not see.
> —HEBREWS 11:1

> Faith is the substance of things hoped for, the evidence of things not seen.
> —HEBREWS 11:1, NKJV

The faith you want to believe in and rely upon must come directly from God. It must come to your spirit personally, not from some perceived promise in the Bible, regardless of how good the promise appears and how much we desire God's intervention. Paul stated the following, "Faith comes by hearing, and hearing by the word of God" (Rom. 10:17, NKJV). What Paul is saying is that learning and knowing the Word of God, the Scriptures, prepares you to hear from God.[177] In addition, it is this hearing that releases faith in you because you have heard from God, and His Word is always reliable. As mentioned previously, faith is dependent on knowing Him and developing a trust in Him based on experience.[178] You must have a certainty in your spirit, a knowing within your spirit, without even a shadow of doubt. You then can expect the manifestation.

It is important to remember that God can say no! You need to seek His answer regardless of what it is and do not believe that silence indicates a denial. However, if you do not ever hear an answer from God, that really could be the problem. Hearing involves your spirit, not just your mind or emotions. As Matthew 22:37 states, when we love God, we are supposed to "love the Lord your God with all your heart and with all your soul and with all your mind." Can we worship or pray to Him with anything less?

Thus, faith is more than thinking about a possibility; it is when there is a knowing or certainty in your spirit that it will be. One of the best examples in the Gospels of what faith is all about is when the woman who had a long history of bleeding knew that if she touched Jesus' robe she would be healed (Luke 8:43–48). To her, this healing was not a mere possibility, but a certainty. Many people brushed up against His robe, but no other person was mentioned as being healed. She had the confidence that came from knowing as truth that she would be healed if she touched His robe. This knowing in your spirit is the difference between true faith and merely relying on hope. This concept may appear to be merely an argument about semantics, but those who know Jesus can also know when God has spoken and faith can be released, rather than merely relying on mental hopes and assumed promises.

---

177 It is the knowing of the Word within your heart, not a memorization, that is important. In fact, memorization can be counterproductive because you can confuse your memory with the Holy Spirit. Jesus said the Holy Spirit would help you recall the Word when you need it. It is possible that excessive memorization can also be the work of a religious spirit.

178 Faith begins with God speaking to your spirit. Your desires, regardless of how good the outcome would be, are not the same as faith. Therefore, do not feel guilty about your faith being inadequate merely because your desire does not occur. If you know Jesus, He can speak the words that create faith.

Our ability to be able to release or exercise faith is directly dependent on:

- the closeness of our relationship with Jesus,
- the depth of our love of Jesus, and
- the maturity of our spirit.

These are all related to each other, and they are dependent on our efforts. Your faith grows over time and with experience. It is not instantaneous. In essence, your maturity, love, and closeness with Jesus increase with the sanctification process. You prepare your spirit through study and prayer, but above all with a humble spirit, recognizing that the process has little to do with an intellectual study of the Bible and more on communicating with Jesus. Mostly we must wait, listen, and be patient (Luke 8:15)![179]

LIFE'S PROBLEMS OCCUR WITH GOD'S PERMISSION

In general, the above statement is true because we are all in the Era of Faith and because we are not drones or programmed robots in a cause-and-effect existence created by God. However, to blame God for adversity is wrong. It is life! It is a composition developed from or due to many factors, including our choices, as well as the choices of others. In addition to making life even more complex, it sometimes involves events that are caused directly or indirectly by demonic spirits. Why does God not solve every bad thing in our life? If God did get involved in every problem, we would no longer be in an era of faith. Our lives would not be the evidence that proves God's love and justice.

IS GOD RESPONSIBLE FOR OUR TROUBLES?

Man generally believes that there is a cause-and-effect existence and that there will be rewards and punishment that are the consequences of our actions. In the past era under the Law, biblical references outlined a system of punishment for deeds that had broken God's laws, which were labeled as sin. Rewards, both while alive and in the hereafter, were obtained through right behavior. Under the Law, a major purpose of one's life was to determine all of the rules and laws concerning our behavior that God required in order to avoid bad times and to reap good things, like wealth and health. It was not, however, exclusively dependent on man's relationship with God.

---

179 This process is never ending. Expect it to take the rest of your life. The process is on the Lord's schedule and thus, it could depend on what the Lord would have you do, if anything, with the wisdom that comes from the experience.

Throughout the Old Testament, this pattern is very evident. However, because of Jesus, we moved into a different era, an era of faith that affects our spirit and, as a result, also influences our actions. Because of our fleshly nature, we still sometimes revert back into the belief that God is punishing us because of something we have done. In those instances, we may struggle to determine what the problem is and how to correct it. While there is always cause to examine one's heart and actions, it is important to remember that in the present era, bad things happen because of Satan, evil spirits, the desires of our flesh nature, poor and inadequately informed choices, and the actions of others.[180] People's desire is to avoid bad things, but unfortunately, we still think of using Old Testament concepts.

Imagine for a moment if God, regardless of the state of our spirit, had the responsibility of preventing all bad things from happening to us.[181] To do this, God would have to control our actions, even our thoughts. We would not even become trained or learn from experiences because nothing bad would happen that would cause us to learn. We simply would not entertain a thought that could possibly have a bad consequence. The entire world would conform to a set pattern of behavior. Thus, there would be no free will. Without free will, there would be no faith and no relationship. Jesus wants your choice to believe and follow Him to be an exercise of your independent will, not because of pressure from relatives, your community, or habits from childhood. If it is not an independent freewill choice, then it is not based solely upon faith. If there is not a completely independent decision, it is not of God, because faith cannot exist. Belief might exist, but that is not the same as faith and they are often confused. For example, if you believe in certain ideas because you are expected to believe them or have been trained to believe them, you will not have faith in your spirit, but merely belief in you mind. Christianity is based upon a spiritual condition.

God did not create us to be mindless creatures without the possibility of making wrong decisions. This is important to understand because if God does not seek absolute, tyrannical control over our flesh activities, why do some religions attempt to do so? There should be no doubt that if God wanted to control us, He could. If He wanted a trained pet, He could have instituted a program

---

180 Since we do not have the ability to accurately contemplate in each circumstance the likelihood that a certain choice will result in a specific desired outcome, we cannot help but make "poor" choices, if we reflectively look back.

181 This is something He did not do for the angels. (See 2 Peter 2:4.) Bad things do not only happen to bad people. It rains on the just and the unjust (Matt. 5:45, NKJV).

of intensive reward and punishment, the effect of which would be to eliminate free will and faith. Christianity, on the other hand, does not attempt to control man's actions. Instead, its focus is upon the spirit. Whenever organized religion sets forth laws that control behavior in an effort to please God or a god, the deity being worshiped is an anti-God. It is merely man's ideas or those inspired from Satan that try to counter the only way God has established for us to please Him, namely, having faith in Jesus and developing the relationship with Him that results from that faith. Of course, Satan is fully behind these anti-Christ activities. Satan wants to prove that man cannot rely on faith to change his spirit into the likeness of Jesus.

DOES GOD TAKE A PERSON'S LIFE?

When someone dies, do we believe that God has taken him or her? Do we evaluate the situation and decide that if the death appears to be a merciful act then it must have been God's intervention? Do we evaluate a child's death and a terminally ill cancer patient equally? Or, do we accuse God of being responsible for the child's life?

These can be complex questions if you fail to understand the nature of God. Most of the time, death happens by accidents, diseases, or from the body wearing out. All will die, and there is an upper limit of longevity for the body's organs, which do not regenerate. We are subject to life and all of its problems, which may be caused by various circumstances as well as our own decisions. The exercise of faith, if it exists and when properly understood, can also alter some events that affect our life.[182]

We know that God is merciful, but we cannot expect God, on His own, to begin to intervene in our life in difficult situations we would rather not experience. This is particularly true when we are in an era of faith. Because we are no longer in a system of reward and punishment for our activities, God does not hover over us protecting us from the adverse effects of life. Strangers and even friends will make decisions that harm us. People will cause accidents. We are sometimes careless. These situations bring about many of life's problems that adversely affect us. Through all of this, God is there to help us overcome and mature.[183]

In all things, there is one thing that is true—God loves us. He does not cause the death of innocent children, but He also cannot be expected to create

---

182   Faith, as discussed previously, involves a situation of interaction of God with man.

183   Sadly, most of us will experience grief over the loss of a loved one. God understands our grief, and He is there for us. We should not, however, blame God in any way for our loss.

a protective covering that surrounds them and protects them from all harm. Clearly, God can intervene and prevent harm to an innocent person. However, it should not be expected as a matter of course. Nonetheless, God does not take people.[184] To accuse God of taking or causing the death of a child defames God's character. It is important to remember that if anyone, especially a child, dies, it is not due to someone's not having prayed enough or having inadequate faith.[185]

ARE YOUR DAYS PREDETERMINED BY GOD?

While God knows at any moment in time the probable time of your death, you must remember that you will make choices that may lengthen or shorten your life span.[186] There is less likelihood that a decision will have an immediate affect on your life span. However, it does happen occasionally.

We, as people, have difficulty grasping the fact that God is not controlled or limited by time. It is a gross error to blame God for what we consider someone's short or tragic life. Once born, we are destined to die. Our life before we die is controlled by a host of factors, including our parents, our genes, choices we make, other people's choices, the impacts of the spiritual world on us and others, and the world's assortment of diseases. In other words, it is life! How can we blame God for anything?

Thus, your days are not numbered or predetermined by God. Likewise, your occupation, fame, wealth, or anything else is not predetermined by God, either.[187] Instead, much of your life is influenced by your own free-will

---

184 Sometimes we may like for Him to take them when a person is suffering. However, generally the person must release his own spirit.

185 Jesus indicated that faith could move mountains. This could occur, but, only if we have the mind of Christ.

186 If you were God, you would know with a perfect degree of mathematical certainty what potential decisions could be made by an individual based upon a lifetime of experiences, emotions, and desires being intertwined to determine both the major and minor decisions. Thus, God "sees" into the future because He knows all possible scenarios and how He will respond. This was also known before any creation. He knew and loved us before we were born.

187 One can have a calling by God, but it is still within your will whether or not you follow that calling. Technically, a calling can be either secular or ministerial. It is believed to be inspired by God. Often, in the secular arena, one will have talents that enable him or her to be successful. In the ministerial arena, success is not measured by outward signs but by one's ability to be led by God. Some people enter ministry careers or volunteer opportunities out of a religious spirit. These individuals will become burned out and perceive themselves as failures. However, they should not because they were not called by God in the first place.

choices. Obviously, there are obstacles that sometimes cannot be overcome. Sometimes we say that God has given us a talent or a certain ability. While that is true, God also gives special abilities when He has actually called you into a work of His. Generally, however, our own choices, within the framework of our opportunities, are what shape our destiny, and they are created from our genes, family, education, and the immediate world we live in. Our life is not predetermined, meaning controlled by God, as if we had a fixed course to travel and experiences that He prescribed for us before time began.

Forgiveness

There are three groups of people in our lives: our friends, our enemies, and those who are neither. By far the largest group contains those who are neutral to us. They are unaware of our existence and just go about living their lives, and their contact with us is incidental. Generally, we have little contact with those who are our enemies because we tend to avoid them when we can. However, when we do encounter them, their impact on us can be stressful.

For our friends and brothers, Jesus said, "If your brother sins, rebuke him, and if he repents, forgive him. If he sins against you seven times in a day, and seven times comes back to you and says, 'I repent,' forgive him" (Luke 17:3–4). In a parable, Jesus gave an example of a servant who was forgiven of his debt to his master but would not forgive a debt owed him. Jesus used this parable as a warning that God would not forgive us unless we forgave our brothers. He said, "This is how my heavenly Father will treat each of you unless you forgive your brother from your heart" (Matt. 18:35). However, notice that if the brother will not repent, measures that are more drastic are employed. Jesus said:

> If your brother sins against you, go and show him his fault, just between the two of you. If he listens to you, you have won your brother over. But if he will not listen, take one or two others along, so that "every matter may be established by the testimony of two or three witnesses." If he refuses to listen to them, tell it to the church; and if he refuses to listen even to the church, treat him as you would a pagan or a tax collector. I tell you the truth, whatever you bind on earth will be bound in heaven, and whatever you loose on earth will be loosed in heaven.
> —MATTHEW 18:15–18

Thus, unrepentant brothers who refuse to respond to godly counsel and alter their rebellious behavior should be shunned, not welcomed back into the assembly of believers. Later, Paul would take a similar approach in his teaching.

However, it would be a rare case, probably where a person had a rebellious and sinful spirit (1 Cor. 5:5).

For enemies, Jesus had a different approach.

> You have heard that it was said, "Eye for eye, and tooth for tooth." But I tell you, Do not resist an evil person. If someone strikes you on the right cheek, turn to him the other also. And if someone wants to sue you and take your tunic, let him have your cloak as well. If someone forces you to go one mile, go with him two miles. Give to the one who asks you, and do not turn away from the one who wants to borrow from you. You have heard that it was said, "Love your neighbor and hate your enemy." But I tell you: Love your enemies and pray for those who persecute you, that you may be sons of your Father in heaven.
>
> —MATTHEW 5:38–45

You should be aware that Jesus was addressing a society controlled by the Old Testament principles (Exod. 21:24; Lev. 24:21; Deut. 19:21). It was a social and legal system of retaliation, in like kind, as a means of meting out justice. Jesus was trying to create within them a new way of thinking.

In our society, we have a legal system that does not foster vengeance.[188] Nevertheless, does this mean that we do not defend ourselves or allow evil to be perpetrated and unpunished? Are we not our brother's keeper? Do we have an obligation to fight evil with justice? Could our failure to do anything be construed to mean we condone evil? Paul said to hate what is evil (Rom. 12:9), however, we do not repay evil with evil (Rom. 12:17). We do not take revenge (Rom. 12:19). First Corinthians 13:6–7 says, "Love does not delight in evil but rejoices with the truth. It always protects, always trusts, always hopes, always perseveres." Therefore, when it comes to our enemies, we try to get along, not retaliating but praying for them, that their hearts would change by the power of Jesus. Sometimes we may need to bind the evil spirits that may be involved.

What, then, did Jesus mean when he said, "For if you forgive men when they sin against you, your heavenly Father will also forgive you, But if you do not forgive men their sins, your Father will not forgive your sins" (Matt. 6:14–15).

---

188 A separate legal system, separate from religious laws that govern our actions, is important in that it allows us to let the law take care of the lawless and for Christianity to deal with our spirit. In developing countries without a strong legal system, people often will trade their freedom for a religious system that brings law and order to their society. Thus, they accept bondage for peace. Clearly this is satanic because it prevents faith from being released through a relationship with Jesus.

Is repentance still a requirement for God, but not for those who sin against us? In all likelihood, Jesus knew that your enemies would seldom ask for forgiveness. He also knew that the Father requires repentance before He will forgive us. Consequently, it would appear consistent if our forgiveness must always be predicated upon some form of repentance from those who sin against us (Luke 17:3–4). However, considering that this is not very likely to occur, we do not let anger or hate enter our spirit about the situation. Hopefully, this does not happen very often. If you are trying to live in peace, and you believe others are sinning against you too often, perhaps there is something wrong in your judgment of the circumstances. Perhaps there is a spirit within you that needs to be dealt with.[189]

In light of what Jesus said about forgiveness, there is one additional statement He made after His resurrection. In John 20:23, He said, "If you forgive anyone his sins, they are forgiven; if you do not forgive them, they are not forgiven." The New King James Version says, "If you forgive the sins of any, they are forgiven them; if you retain the sins of any, they are retained." Thus, Jesus gave the option and even implied that there could be situations where you would not forgive someone's sin. He did not give the parameters, but probably a lack of repentance is one of them. We know that blasphemy of the Holy Spirit is unforgiveable. Jesus mentioned several instances where the lambs (new Christians) are abused or intentionally misled and the consequences are severe. (See Matthew 18:6; 2 Peter 2:1.) Perhaps sins against us personally, under the previously mentioned circumstances, would be forgiven.

There is a mistaken belief concerning judging and forgiveness. That is, we are not to judge anyone, because if we don't judge we can avoid being judged ourselves. (See Matthew 7:1.) That is wrong. God will judge us all.

However, we are called upon to judge good from evil. Paul said the saints will judge the world and that those who are mature will be able to discern good and evil. (See 1 Corinthians 6:2; Hebrews 5:14.) We are not to run away from responsibility nor from recognizing evil. How could you correct your brother if you never judged? We basically are cautioned about being a hypocrite by judging others with a standard we would not want applied to us. We are always to judge the actions of others, without hypocrisy, and if possible examine their motives when revealed by the Holy Spirit. How would people know their actions are wrong if no one told them? It is true, however, that the manner of correction is very important, and it is a difficult situation not handled well by most

---

189 The statement regarding Jesus forgiving people from the cross in Luke 23:34 does not appear in many ancient manuscripts. If Jesus actually said this, He was probably referring to the Romans, not the Jews, since Jesus told Pilate that they had a great sin (John 19:11).

people. It must be done with love for the spirit of the person. Often, people do not correct others with a pure motive or loving manner.

SUMMARY OF MAJOR POINTS

- God never has to drive anyone. Thus, if you feel under a compulsion or obligation, it is not from God. He also does not test a Christian, even indirectly through Satan. Satan does that on his own if he thinks he will win.
- Temptations help us know the areas within us that need to be changed. Therefore, treat them as information about our weaknesses that need to be dealt with. During the sanctification process, we will overcome the weakness within us that allows temptations to occur.
- Tithing is not a requirement of God for Christians. We should be led by the Holy Spirit in all areas relating to the management of money.
- Our good deeds should be motivated by the love that flows from our spirit. They are not to be performed for the approval of God or man.
- The level of faith we have is directly proportional to our love and the depth of our relationship with Jesus. It is a matter between the individual and Jesus.
- Everyone's life will have problems. God is not the source of our problems, even indirectly. God does not take people's lives, and one's life span is not fixed by God. The exercise of one's own free well, as well as that of other people, can affect many factors and influence your life.
- Forgiving our brother when he sins against us is predicated upon a repentant spirit on their part. If we are wronged by our enemies, we should communicate our feelings if it might clear up the situation and improve the relationship. However, keep in mind that if one does not address the problem, that inaction could be construed as condoning the evil act.

9

DISPENSATIONALISM AND THE RAPTURE

WHERE DID THIS IDEA COME FROM?

MAN LIKES TO believe he can solve mysteries, such as, when will the second coming of Jesus occur? He believes this mystery can be solved if he can study the Bible and ancient history adequately.

However, there is an underlying assumption that many make, namely, that there is a certain event that Christians must collectively perform in order to bring about the return of Jesus. Dispensationalists believe that God deals with mankind according to different relationship patterns that are narrow in scope. Thus, the Era of Faith brought about through Jesus is subdivided into distinct periods. They believe that the last phase is the millennial reign of Jesus. At the core of their beliefs is that the Jews get another chance to accept Jesus before He returns. This premise, on its surface, does not appear too bad. However, it is based upon speculation regarding the Book of Revelation. Jesus said only the Father knows when He will return (Matt. 24:36).

The timing of His return could also involve the maturity of the church and its meeting some unknown standard such as when Jesus finds an adequate amount of faith on the earth (Luke 18:8), when the Great Commission is completed, or simply after the passage of a set amount of time. Alternatively, it could be when the world contains a certain percentage of Christians. In fact, early Christianity believed that when a certain number of Christians existed (counting both those who had died as well as those alive on the earth), Jesus would return. Another theory is that Jesus will return when every single person on the earth over the age of accountability has heard the message of the gospel. More than likely, it is something altogether different.

This doctrine is similar to another concept some religious groups believe that states that after death those who did not accept Jesus during their lives will get a second chance after seeing the alternative. Those that believe there is a second chance after their death fail to consider the implication of what Jesus

meant when He said, "You are from below; I am from above. You are of this
world; I am not of this world. I told you that you would die in your sins; if you
do not believe that I am [the one I claim to be], you will indeed die in your
sins" (John 8:23–24). Thus, when one dies a sinner, the automatic destination
for their soul is hell. Only if you are righteous, meaning saved by your belief
and faith in Jesus, will you see heaven after your death. The key is whether or
not you die in your sin, as a sinner.

Jesus came to bring salvation as well as to encourage us to change our spirits.
If Jesus merely brought salvation and you had an opportunity to accept Him
after your death, you would never need to change; sin would be rewarded. This
theory, called universalism, appears to be based upon a concept that there is
either no hell or, if it does exist, no humans are in it, because God is so good
that no one will be punished. This doctrine implies that there is a temporary
place where man gets another chance to believe in Jesus as his Savior, even if
he rejected Christ during his lifetime. But this is not what Jesus dying for all
means. Jesus basically said the destination of all men is hell, because all men
are sinners until and unless Christ is their Savior (John 8:23–24; 14:6). He also
said in Mark 16:16 that unless one believes in Him and is baptized, he will not
be saved.

The word *dispensation* comes from Ephesians 3:2–4 (KJV), but the doctrine
of dispensationalism started in approximately 1810–1820, when a young girl in
Scotland prophesied that there was going to be a multi-step process in Jesus'
return. It is now related to the concept of the Rapture. Some Christian religious
leaders at that time believed that this was the concept that could explain the
meaning of the missing period of time in Daniel 9:26–27, the gap between the
sixty-ninth and seventieth week, and the Book of Revelation.

In approximately 1840, John N. Darby concluded that man's relationship with
God was reflected in seven eras, or dispensations.[190] They are the following:

1. The pre-Flood period

2. Noah's time

3. Abraham's time

4. Israel's time up to Jesus

5. The era of the Gentiles

---

190 Darby came to believe in a future salvation and restoration of national Israel in which Israel
would enjoy earthly blessings because of a reversion to the Law after the church was gone. One
problem that Darby's position does not consider is Paul's statement that the Christian is the true Jew
(Rom. 2:28). That being the case, Christ's church is the true Israel.

6. The era of the Spirit
7. The Millennium

Since then, others have come up with a similar breakdown. While a reflection on history indicates that various stages or eras can be identified over the course of the relationship between man and God, they are not as Darby concluded. Consider the following periods, which are based upon man's various states of sin and God's interaction with man. (See Chapter 2 for a more detailed description of each age.) There could be six periods for man on Earth. The seventh, not shown, will be in the kingdom of God.

- Garden—In our sinless state we enjoyed the maximum relationship with God while on Earth.
- Garden to the Flood—The wickedness of man increases. This period was approximately 1,650 years long.
- The Flood to Abraham—Wickedness returns after the flood. This period lasted approximately 430 years.
- Abraham to the Exodus—Abraham, a man of faith, initiates a new beginning when God makes a covenant with him because of his walk of faith. It spanned approximately 430 years.
- The Exodus to Jesus—Called the Era of the Law, this period lasted approximately 1,500 years.
- Jesus to the present—We are currently in the Era of Faith under a new covenant that began two thousand years ago.

Another approach would be to consider the Garden experience as merely setting the foundation. In this approach, the period from the Garden of Eden to the Exodus is classified simply as the period before the Law. The second period, from Moses to Jesus, marks the period of the Law. The third, from Jesus to the end of the earth as we know it, is the period of faith.

As you can see, one can pretty much make up his own period breakdown depending on the outcome he wants. So, one should not get too technical about the number of periods because it leads to legalism.

Remember, what we are examining is how God is proving and justifying His responses to Lucifer and the angels' rebellion. The problem with dispensationalism is that it implies that God always meant to deal with man under a system of laws, such that salvation by faith in Jesus as the risen Son of God is not necessary for those who are of the Jewish faith.[191] Again, faith, not the Law, was always the primary goal.[192] The period of the Law merely proves that the Law does not work as a means of salvation. If one accepts this, then he or she will recognize that dispensationalism is an erroneous concept that minimizes Jesus. Jesus is not "an option." One's interpretation of Revelation is incorrect if somehow it reinstitutes the Law, even for a short period.[193]

In effect, the concept of dispensationalism diminishes Jesus to merely being the means of salvation for the non-Jew. This results from a concept that lifts up the Jewish people as being exempt from anything new from God, unless it meets their expectations and interpretations of messianic prophesy. While it is important to note that there is no justification for anyone, Christian or otherwise, to harbor anti-Semitic feelings, it must nonetheless be pointed out that Paul, after discussing Jews and Gentiles, said that God does not show favoritism; the same standards apply for each group (Rom. 2:11). There is a major problem in a belief that Jews have a special and permanent relationship with God that is superior to His relationship with the Gentiles and minimizes the relationship the rest of the world has with Jesus.

It appears odd that Darby, and others that followed, would want to revere the Jews when Paul said that Christians are Abraham's seed and heir to God's promise to Abraham (Gal. 3:29) and that the Christian is the true Jew (Rom. 2:28–29). That being the case, Christ's church is the true nation of Israel. Jesus hinted that they would no longer be special in Matthew 8:11–12. This passage indicates that although many Jews would join Abraham, Isaac, and Jacob at a feast in the kingdom of heaven, their heritage alone will not prevent them from being thrown into darkness after judgment.

It is interesting that Christianity originally began as a sect of Judaism. For a few years there even appeared to be the idea in the first churches in Jerusalem that it should maintain many of the Jewish traditions. However, soon after James was beheaded (A.D. 44 or 45) and Paul began his ministry to the

---

191 Some would argue that the current view is called progressive dispensationalism, and it is different from the view of theologian C. I. Scofield, which stated that the church interrupted God's dealings with Israel. The progressives believe that the church is for the non-Jew and that God's covenant with Israel, contained in the Old Testament, is still valid for the Jews. They still lift the Law above Jesus.

192 Remember, Abraham was a man of faith. Moses could also be called a man of faith. Then the Law came. Except for a few prophets, are there any notable men who are cited as great men of faith while under the law?

193 There are no other dispensations in which Jesus is merely an option. He was the fulfillment of the Law. One cannot demean Him by now raising the Jewish people into a special class that is exempt from a requirement of faith. Does this not raise the Law above Jesus?

Gentiles, many of the apostles went into other regions throughout the Middle East, India, China, Russia, Europe, and perhaps Britain. The Jews had an opportunity to become Christians, and many did. However, the Jewish religious leaders would not accept Christ, and they had control over most of the people. Soon they began to persecute Christians.

What Did Jesus Say?

Jesus seemed to indicate that there is a new era, a change from the Law, rather than an intermission.

> The law and the prophets were until John. Since that time the kingdom of God has been preached, and everyone is pressing into it. And it is easier for heaven and earth to pass away than for one tittle of the law to fail.
>
> —Luke 16:16, nkjv

He said earlier that He came to fulfill the Law, not to merely fulfill it for the Gentiles. If He came to fulfill it, why is it, and the bondage associated with it, still applicable?

> Do not think that I have come to abolish the Law or the Prophets; I have not come to abolish them but to fulfill them.
>
> —Matthew 5:17

Jesus gave a parable that appears to dispel the idea that the Jews can ignore the Christian movement and think they will be welcomed in heaven.

> And He said to them, Strive to enter through the narrow gate,[194] for many, I say to you, will seek to enter and will not be able. When once the Master of the house has risen up and shut the door, and you begin to stand outside and knock at the door, saying, "Lord, Lord, open for us," and He will answer and say to you, "I do not know you, where you are from," then you will begin to say, "We ate and drank in Your presence, and You taught in our streets." But He will say, "I tell you I do not know you, where you are from. Depart from Me, all you workers of iniquity." There will be weeping and gnashing of teeth, when you see Abraham and Isaac and Jacob and all the prophets in the kingdom

---

194 If the narrow gate is being born again; if the Master of the house is the Father; and if those that see Abraham, Isaac, and Jacob, are Jews, they will be thrust out, but the rest of the world (Gentiles who have been saved by Christ) will sit down in the kingdom of God.

of God, and yourselves thrust out. They will come from the east and the west, from the north and the south, and sit down in the kingdom of God. And indeed there are last who will be first, and there are first who will be last."

—LUKE 13:23–30, NKJV

Finally, Jesus said in Matthew 21:43–44 (NKJV), "Therefore I say to you, the kingdom of God will be taken from you and given to a nation bearing the fruits of it. And whoever falls on this stone will be broken; but on whomever it falls, it will grind him to powder." Wasn't Jesus saying that the kingdom of God would be taken from the those under the Law?

WHAT DID PAUL SAY?

If the Era of Faith is only for the Gentile and the Era of the Law is for the Jew, then there would be support for Darby's dispensationalist theory. However, if Jesus came to move humanity into a new era by changing man's spirit, replacing the Law that merely shaped our behavior, then perhaps Paul best explained this concept.

In one of his first letters, Galatians,[195] he wrote, "I want you to know, brothers, that the gospel I preached is not something that man made up. I did not receive it from any man, nor was I taught it; rather, I received it by revelation from Jesus Christ" (Gal. 1:11–12). In all likelihood, the revelation occurred when he was in Arabia for three years soon after his conversion (Gal. 1:15–18). In particular, he wrote that his purpose was "to reveal his Son [in me] so that I might preach him among the Gentiles" (Gal. 1:16, NKJV).[196]

Approximately six years later, in his letter to the Romans, he summed up the issue of whether the Law or Christ would bring salvation in one sentence: "The righteous will live by faith" (Rom. 1:17; quoted from Hab. 2:4, written approximately six hundred years before the Incarnation). Later in the letter, Paul clearly states that "a man is justified by faith apart from observing the law. Is God the God of Jews only? Is he not the God of Gentiles too? Yes, of Gentiles too, since there is only one God, who will justify the circumcised by faith and the uncircumcised through that same faith" (Rom. 3:28–30). Thus, humanity,

---

195 Galatians was likely written in approximately A.D. 49, though some argue it was written six to seven years later.

196 Note that Paul did not say "to me," but "in me." This perhaps meant that Paul had more than an apparition of Christ, but rather an extensive revelation about and from Jesus, including His purposes. Because of Paul's intellect, his extensive rabbinical training, and the fact that he could write well, he had a greater responsibility to carry the message beyond the local Jewish nation.

including the Jewish nation, is no longer justified by observing the Law but by faith in Jesus only. Paul does not even hint that God had two different sets of criteria for salvation, one method for the Jews and another method for everyone else. In fact, he made it clear that the only way for us to become righteous is through Jesus when he stated, "But now a righteousness from God, apart from law, has been made known, to which the Law and the Prophets testify. This righteousness from God comes through faith in Jesus Christ to all who believe. There is no difference, for all have sinned and fall short of the glory of God" (Rom. 3:21–23).

To clarify why the Jews' observance of the Law had previously been ineffective, he stated the reason was "because they pursued it not by faith but as if it were by works" (Rom. 9:32). He had previously stated this in his letter to the Galatians when he wrote, "We who are Jews by birth and not 'Gentile sinners' know that a man is not justified by observing the law, but by faith in Jesus Christ. So we, too, have put our faith in Christ Jesus that we may be justified by faith in Christ and not by observing the law, because by observing the law no one will be justified" (Gal. 2:15–16).

It was simply explained by Paul that, "Before this faith came, we were held prisoners by the law, locked up until faith should be revealed. So the law was put in charge to lead us to Christ that we might be justified by faith. Now that faith has come, we are no longer under the supervision of the law" (Gal. 3:23–25). Thus, we are in the Era of Faith. The Law was for a season, but it has been replaced by faith in Jesus. This was stated by Paul in Romans, "But now, by dying to what once bound us, we have been released from the law so that we serve in the new way of the Spirit, and not in the old way of the written code" (Rom. 7:6). One cannot live under the Law and at the same time live by faith. For the Law kills the spirit, but the Holy Spirit gives life to our spirit (2 Cor. 3:6).

If one argues that Christianity is for the Gentiles' salvation only, then why did Paul write, "All who rely on observing the law are under a curse" (Gal. 3:10)? He went on to write, "Christ redeemed us from the curse of the law by becoming a curse for us…He redeemed us in order that the blessing given to Abraham might come to the Gentiles through Christ Jesus, so that by faith we might receive the promise of the Spirit" (Gal. 3:13–14). Therefore, while it is true that salvation was expanded to include all humanity, the method of salvation also became faith in Jesus Christ.

Paul, in Romans 11, wrote to the Jews[197] as well as the Gentiles who had accepted Jesus, particularly those in Rome. He stated that the door was open for the Jews to accept Jesus (vv. 7–12, 23, 31), and that until the "fullness of the Gentiles has come in," Jews would continue to be saved (vv. 25–26).[198] Paul also indicated that Christian Gentiles would still be on the earth until some unknown quantity of Gentiles had been saved. Paul is not saying that all of (national) Israel will be saved, but that both the Jews and Christians who believe in Christ as their Savior will become the new Israel. In Galatians 3:6–9, Paul redefines Israel in the following way:

> Even as Abraham believed God, and it was reckoned unto him for righteousness. Know therefore that they that are of faith, the same are sons of Abraham. And the scripture, foreseeing that God would justify the Gentiles by faith, preached the gospel beforehand unto Abraham, saying, In thee shall all the nations be blessed. So then they that are of faith are blessed with the faithful Abraham. (ASV)

Elsewhere, Paul clearly indicates that it is the existence of Christian Gentiles on Earth that facilitates salvation for the Jews. He makes the statement that because of the observation of the blessings on the Christians, the Jews would be drawn to Christ (Rom. 11:31). For this to occur, Christians have to be present in significant quantities. Thus, there is no time period where Christians have left the earth. Thus, there is no dispensation for the Jew and no Rapture in which the Christians are absent from the earth.

The impact to Christianity from a belief in dispensationalism is the mistaken idea that there is a need to aid national Israel. This idea has also manifested itself through the Rapture theory. The survival of Israel is believed to be the determining cause for Jesus' return. Thus, for example, it is believed that when the original temple in Jerusalem, destroyed by the Romans, is rebuilt, Jesus will return. However, this is based upon a misunderstanding of the Book of Revelation.

---

197 Earlier in his letter, Paul identified the true Jew as one who was circumcised in their heart, not his flesh (Rom. 2:29). However, in chapter 11 he was speaking of those with a Jewish background or heritage who had not accepted Jesus.

198 In 1706, Matthew Henry rejected the concept that any reestablishment of the Jewish temple or priesthood awaited the Jews. (See Matthew Henry, *Complete Commentary on the Whole Bible* [Peabody, MA: Hendrickson Publishers, 2005].)

Revelation[199] contains many symbolic references. Thus, it was never intended to be read literally. If Revelation were meant to be taken literally, then the Holy Spirit would not be as important as He is to our understanding of the Bible. In addition, man could rely on his own intellect, his ability for memory, and perhaps an intense effort of study. Symbolic prophetic words, taken as a literal script of future events, were probably never the intent of John. When, however, it is recognized that there is a large quantity of symbolism in the book, it cannot be taken as only applying to future events because it could also have been a symbolic statement of history during the reign of Nero and others who persecuted the Christians.

The opinions given by experts on what the Book of Revelation indicates about the End Times are merely speculation on a book that contains symbolic imagery 1,900 years old. We will probably never know what John was intending for his contemporary readers to learn from his letter. For example, was John writing about events that had already taken place, or was he writing about the future? Perhaps portraying events that would occur hundreds of years in the future was not his intent. Rather, the letter may have been to help the persecuted victims endure their tribulations with the message that Jesus would prevail.[200]

THE RAPTURE

What does Revelation indicate?

Like the Trinity, *rapture* is not a term used in the Bible.[201] However, is it otherwise indicated?

The primary scriptures used to explain the doctrine about the Rapture are in Paul's first epistle to the Thessalonians and in the Book of Matthew. First Thessalonians 4:16–18 seems to indicate that Jesus will return and that Christians, as well as those already dead, will ascend (be caught up) to the clouds to meet Jesus. The letter was one of Paul's first letters, written in approximately

---

199   Revelation may have been written after the period of Nero, after Jerusalem was destroyed. Alternatively, it may have been written in the middle to late 90s. Revelation was not accepted early on to be part of the Canon of the Church. By A.D. 325, the Bible as we know it was established, except for Revelation. By A.D. 365, it was added by the Western church. (See *Jamieson, Fausset, and Brown's Commentary on the Whole Bible*, Zondervan, 1999.)

200   The churches mentioned in Revelation would have been located in present-day Turkey.

201   Instead, passages like 1 Thessalonians 4:17 use the Greek word *harpazo*, which simply means "caught up." The Latin Vulgate Bible used the term *raptus*, from which we get the English word "rapture."

A.D. 51.[202] Matthew records that Jesus said there would be a gathering of the tares by the angels of the Lord (Matt. 13:37–42). Jesus explained the parable to His disciples. He indicated that while the wheat and tares, the undesirable plants or weeds, would exist side by side, the tares would be removed and cast into the fire at the time of the gathering. In addition, the saints shall view Jesus' return. (See Matthew 24:30–31.) Jesus also said that the elect will be gathered up after natural signs appear in the heavens (Matt. 24:29–31).[203]

When Christians refer to the Rapture, they are usually talking about a two-phase return of Jesus, in which the elect are gathered from the earth and the unsaved are left for a period until the final stage of His second coming. There is no clear record of any of the early church writers mentioning a return of this sort. The earliest clear mention of this theory appear to have been recorded perhaps as early as 1750. These records indicate that the Rapture theory was based on the simple idea that the church would not be around if Satan were actually ruling the world because it would imply that Christians did not have authority delegated from Jesus to war against Satan. Thus, by implication, for Satan to rule, the church must not exist on Earth.

The idea of the two-part rapture first began around 1810–1830. The concept is credited to have begun as an alleged prophecy by Margaret MacDonald, a young girl in Scotland.[204] In this same time period, other church leaders began to preach a message that God would restore the spiritual gifts to the church. Soon, some Christians bean to expect the second coming of Jesus. In this atmosphere, John N. Darby, founder of the Plymouth Brethren, adopted it and began to promote the concept in conjunction with his doctrine about dispensationalism, which he began teaching between 1820 and 1830. Up to that time, it was not reflected in church doctrine of either the Catholics or Protestants. Darby became known as the father of the pre-Tribulation Rapture

---

202 It is clear from this letter and others that Paul and the other church leaders expected Jesus to return in the first century. Immediately after Jesus died, the church in Jerusalem seemed to almost but not completely endorse a communal style of living as if in preparation for His return. Later on, Paul took up collections to help the church in Jerusalem, because they probably had not made prudent long-term plans, just doing enough to get by from day to day (1 Cor. 16:3; Rom. 15:26).

203 The interval of time involved between the natural signs in the skies and the gathering is unknown. (See Matthew 24:29.)

204 The apostle John, however, warned against believing every vision and dream because false prophets existed even during the early church period (1 John 4:1). Many times only those with a mature spirit, discerning the circumstances, can you tell the difference between a move of God and that of the enemy. Satan can counterfeit many things, and Jesus said that many will do miracles in His name but He may not know them (Matt. 7:21–23). Thus, you cannot equate what seem to be "good" works with approval from God of either a person or a message being presented.

movement. In approximately 1870, the doctrine came to the United States. Cyrus I. Scofield, author of the *Scofield Reference Bible* (1909), became a chief proponent of this doctrine.

The basic underlying issue concerns Jews. Is the Jews' covenant with God still valid considering the fact that Jesus said no one could come to the Father except through Him?[205] Dispensationalists believe that there has to be a plan wherein the new covenant does not replace the old covenant but merely creates an option where the Jews will have a special period to accept Jesus.

The underlying problem for Bible scholars is to try to understand what event will trigger Jesus' return. The two-phase return aided Darby in his promotion of the concept of dispensationalism. Man often attempts to reason through Scripture by taking isolated statements and weaving them together into a pattern he can recognize. In this case, Darby has taken a gap mentioned in the book of Daniel and combined it with verses from Revelation. He used these to support the concept of a two-phase return of Jesus. As well as his justification for the Rapture, Darby also supported the belief that the resurgence of the State of Israel and the rebuilding of the temple in Jerusalem are determinate events for establishing when Jesus will return.[206]

From the concept of the Rapture, there have been different theories on when the gathering of the saints will occur. These vary depending on one's belief in whether the church will have to endure the seven years of tribulation that are supposed to occur when Satan is given free reign over the world.

---

205 A general premise is that God's promises are for all eternity and not for a period. Since God knows the future, it would seem that if He is silent about the duration of a promise, it should be assumed that it would expire because conditions change enough to make it no longer valid. Consider this: would God ever put an unconditional time of expiration on a promise when the exercise of man's free will can either shorten or lengthen it's applicably?

206 In approximately 1940, competing theories came into vogue that have as their core belief a restoration of what was believed to be the power of the first century church as well as several other beliefs about the church's ultimate responsibility. One is the belief that the determining factor of when Jesus will return is the subjection of the kingdoms of this world through the work of the church. (This is often referred to as kingdom theology.) Jesus said to preach the gospel of God's kingdom throughout the world as a testimony to all nations (Matt. 24:14), and many believe that until the gospel reaches every part and person of the world, the Rapture will not take place. While Christianity is the largest faith in the world, it is not the majority faith in the world. Many nations do not have a significant testimony that is a witness to them, certainly not with the power that is present with the kingdom of God, as indicated by Paul. (See 1 Corinthians 4:20.)

(See Revelation 11:2).[207] There are three interpretations. First, the most vocal one, promoted by Cyrus I. Scofield in his annotated Bible, published in 1909, is that the church would be removed while Satan ruled the earth during a period when the Jewish Law was reinstituted. This was known as the pre-Tribulation Rapture.

Scofield mentioned the Rapture of the church in a footnote to 1 Thessalonians 4:17. He connected Revelation 7:14 with Daniel 9:27 and the seventieth week of Daniel. He goes on to say (in an annotation to Revelation 7:14) that the Great Tribulation will be followed immediately by the return of Christ. Where is the church during this period? Scofield indicates that the church is not present, although an "election out of Israel will be redeemed with an innumerable multitude of Gentiles." He says the Law, along with sacrifices and worship in the temple, will be reestablished; and it will be a period of unexampled trouble and judgment that will involve the whole earth.

It is the predominate belief concerning the gathering of the saints before Jesus' final return. It reemerged in the 1970s. In fact, many novels have been written based upon the principle that the saints disappear from the earth, leaving the unsaved. It is believed that many of those who accept Jesus during the Tribulation will be martyred. Of course, if the believers are all gone, who will preach to them or tell them about Jesus?

The second belief is that the saints will be caught up in the middle of the two forty-two-month periods. The third belief is that the gathering of the saints will be after the Tribulation period. Jesus' own prayer to the Father asks that the saints not be taken away but that they would be protected (John 17:15–16). Perhaps we have already gone through the Tribulation, because John's writing could have been concerned with the destruction of Jerusalem in A.D. 70 by Rome. In addition, depending on when one believes Revelation was written the Antichrist mentioned in 1 John may have been referring to Nero (late A.D. 60) or Domitian (A.D. 95–96), both of whom were killing Christians during their respective reigns. One can easily believe that John was not speaking of a time hundreds of years in the future but of times that were more contemporary by the use of allegorical and symbolic language that the readers would understand. Remember, John was writing to his contemporaries. He likely wanted them to understand what he was saying yet have his writing pass inspection if read by a Roman. He was probably not focusing on a reader 1,900 years into the future.

---

207 In a literal interpretation, the seven years mentioned are two forty-two-month periods. Some believe that the first forty-two months will consist of peace and the second forty-two months of war. Others believe the entire seven years is continuous.

WHAT DID JESUS SAY?

Jesus is quoted in several places speaking about the End Times. In Mark 13:5–37, Jesus says, without indicating a particular time span, that there would be much turmoil and persecution before He came back. Luke 21:8–36 is a comparable passage, except that it speaks of the destruction of Jerusalem, which actually occurred about forty years later in A.D. 70. Jesus, in speaking of the End Times, said, "And these glad tidings of the kingdom shall be preached in the whole habitable earth, for a witness to all the nations, and then shall come the end. When therefore ye shall see the abomination of desolation, which is spoken of through Daniel the prophet, standing in [what is a] holy place" (Matt. 24:14–15, DNT). The exact meaning of this phrase is unclear because Jesus admitted that He used figurative language at times (John 16:25). Mark 13:24–25 also says that immediately before He comes back, almost simultaneously, the heavens will display unusual signs, such as the sun becoming less bright. He will come in a cloud, along with His angels, who He will send to gather the elect.[208]

However, in the parable in Matthew 13:30, it appears the weeds will be removed before the harvest. In Luke 17:30–35, Jesus said that at His second coming, some would be taken and some would be left. He does not say who will be taken. Is it the tares (weeds), or the elect?

CAN ANYONE, AT THIS TIME, UNDERSTAND REVELATION?

John probably wrote the Book of Revelation in approximately A.D. 90–95. He uses allegorical and symbolic words that had particular meaning to the readers. However, centuries later, the meaning is unclear and can easily be misunderstood. It cannot be understood by applying literal meaning to the words. For example, many people understand the Antichrist as a single human being, rather than merely the Antichrist spirit John had mentioned in the letters known as 1 and 2 John, which were written at the same general time.[209]

---

208 This verse would indicate those who were still alive. In Luke, immediately after speaking on the destruction of Jerusalem, one could conclude that Jesus would immediately return. However, that would only be an assumption, because it is not recorded that He had anything else to say between verses 24 and 25. It seems that Christ purposely did not give any indication of the time interval that would lapse between His ascension and return.

209 The letters of John were probably written before Revelation. It is uncertain whether the apostle John is the author of Revelation. However, most authorities believe he is, even though the writing style is not the same as that of the Gospel.

On the other hand, for example, the term *harlot church* is not actually used in Revelation. The concept is that there will be a church that is so tainted that it is considered an abomination. People have incorrectly labeled the Catholic Church with that brand or label.

Satan has been warring Christ from the time he first became aware that Jesus would be incarnated. He has brought counterfeits and messengers, probably including angels, to create a message or belief that Jesus was not God before He became flesh. In Revelation, John does not actually articulate the Antichrist spirit into a single, clear personification. The seven-headed Beast is mentioned in Revelation 12 and 13, but the meaning is mere speculation to present day readers.

Over the centuries since John was writing, many false doctrines have been created to undermine and negate who Jesus was. Some have even become religions. All of these have been created or inspired by Satan in order to counter faith in Jesus as the only means of salvation.

In addition to the symbolism of terms discussed above, such as *antichrist*, other symbolism concerning numbers has caused some confusion and misunderstanding. For example, the symbolic use of the terms 144,000 and one thousand years. These had meaning to the author, but that meaning is not clear to the current readers, that is, unless we start speculating. This may explain why it took so long (nearly one hundred years) for the book to be accepted as canonical by the Western church.

Over the last 150 years, the basic, underlying dispute that has generated much discussion has been over the millennial (one thousand-year) reign of Christ. (See Revelation 20:7.) One view is that that the Rapture would take place first, followed by the Tribulation and then the one thousand-year reign. However, this view appears to conflict with Jesus' statements in Matthew 24, Mark 13, and Luke 21. The second view is that the Rapture occurs sometime between the start of Tribulation and the millennial reign of Christ. The third view, a doctrine called amillennialism, which has existed since the founding of the early church until approximately 1850, was that we have already had the Tribulation, probably the Roman persecution of Christians from A.D. 65–95 (which was before Revelation was written), and we are now in the one thousand-year reign of Christ awaiting His second coming. With this doctrine, there is no Rapture, only the return of Jesus and the "separation of the wheat and tares."

The doctrine of amillennialism conflicts with Darby's concept of dispensationalism, which holds that nothing begins in the end-time countdown until after the temple in Jerusalem is rebuilt from the destruction in A.D. 70 by the Romans. In addition, according to Darby, the Second Coming does not occur until a number of Jews convert to Christianity.[210]

As mentioned elsewhere, Christians often come up with ideas that place them in the center of whatever needs to occur before Jesus will return. It can involve some action that is either concrete, such as rebuilding a temple, or less tangible, such as overcoming Satan and taking control over the dominions he rules. Perhaps, however, if it does depend in some way upon Christians, the tasks have already been communicated by Jesus and Paul, such as preaching the gospel[211] throughout the world and becoming more like Jesus through the sanctification process so the message is the witness of our lives. At some point that God has established, this phase of man's relationship with God will be finished.

DANGERS FOR BELIEVERS IN THE RAPTURE

- It creates a false hope of a second chance.
- They put emphasis on date-setting instead of preparedness by maturing.
- It sets the stage for a reign of national Israel. If God is no respecter of people, why would God give Jews two alternatives or opportunities for salvation and everyone else only one chance?

Since approximately 1940, other doctrines have emerged. The essential premise is that the church's actions will be the determining factor for when Jesus returns. Some believe that the church will demonstrate through the delegated power of

---

210   While we hope and desire that everyone would come to accept Jesus, Jesus indicated that this would not happen. (See John 5:39–40.)

211   One must be concerned for the millions of people who are born into a religious system that prevents them from knowing Christ. It is clear that our efforts up to this time have not been effective. Our witness has not generally been with the power and gifts of the Holy Spirit; it has mostly been with words. Some have been able to respond, but those in bondage need the encouragement to break free from their religious, social, and familial bondage. Perhaps if we became more like Jesus, the Holy Spirit would allow His mercy and power to flow through us. The missionary work of spreading the gospel is great, but seldom has it met the level of Smith Wigglesworth's ministry. We need more like him. For a complete reference of Smith Wigglesworth's sermons, see *Smith Wigglesworth: The Complete Collection of His Life Teachings*, ed. Roberts Liardon (Tulsa, OK: Albury Publications, 1996). For his biography, see *Wigglesworth: The Complete Story*, ed. Julian Wilson (Colorado, CO: Authentic Publishing, 2004).

God that the church has rule or dominion over Satan. Others believe that individuals will become anointed of God and they will demonstrate with signs, wonders, and miracles, similar to the work of the apostles, that the message of Jesus is the true message of God. Perhaps, however, the timing of the return of Jesus has something to do with spreading the gospel as a witness of the kingdom of God throughout the entire world. Shouldn't we also be concerned about maturing as Christians? Perhaps it is the adequate witness of the mature Christian that has yet to be demonstrated.

SUMMARY OF MAJOR POINTS

- Dispensationalism is an erroneous concept that treats the Jews as a special people who can rely on the Law for their salvation while the saints are on the earth but would be required to turn to Christ during the Tribulation period if they desire salvation. It is unclear how this would occur since no one would be around to preach or witness.
- The concept is not supported by Paul and has the affect of elevating the Law above God's sacrifice and atonement for the repentant believer's sin.
- The doctrine of the Rapture as a two-step return of Jesus is not supported by Jesus' teachings or Paul's writings. It complements the dispensationalist theology, however.
- The Rapture concept attempts to interpret the Books of Revelation and Daniel together, with each allegedly supporting the other. The Book of Revelation contains many allegorical and symbolic terms that a present day reader can only speculate on their meaning. To make and adopt doctrines and beliefs on speculative meanings that divert the church from its mission is a mistake.

10

OTHER INFORMATION YOU SHOULD KNOW

WHAT IS THE KINGDOM OF GOD?

THERE IS SOME confusion over the phrases *kingdom of God* and *kingdom of heaven*. Matthew used, in citing Jesus' words, the phrase *kingdom of heaven* approximately thirty-one times, while the other Gospel writers did not use it at all.[212] It has been said that Matthew, who was writing to a primarily Jewish reader, avoided the phrase *kingdom of God*. Actually, however, he does use the phrase approximately five times when restating what Jesus said. Other Gospel writers wrote often about Jesus' teachings on the kingdom of God. Luke indicated that the people, perhaps Jesus' disciples, were unclear about when the kingdom of God would appear (19:11), so Jesus indicated that it would not become evident until after His death and resurrection (22:18).

Most of the time when Jesus referred to the kingdom of God, He was referring to the potential of an intangible spiritual existence within us that interacts with that part of the kingdom that is in others, as well as with God (Luke 17:21). Jesus said worldly cares and wealth would make it difficult to enter (Matt. 19:24; Mark 10:23). In fact, you can only receive it as a little child (Mark 10:15). In other words, pride will keep you from entering the kingdom of God. Jesus also said that it starts small, like a seed, and grows large like a tree such that it provides shelter for the weak (Mark 4:26–32; Luke 13:18–21). It does not come with observation (Luke 17:20). And, you have to be reborn of the spirit to enter (John 3:3–6). According to Paul, within this kingdom there exists the potential to affect, influence, and change both the spiritual world as well as the physical, visible world (1 Cor. 4:20). One of the evidences that one exists in the

---

212 The International Standard Version does use it in Luke 7:28. Neither the New International Version, New King James Version, nor the King James Version uses the phrase, except in Matthew. Mark may not actually have been there to hear the words. John was writing almost thirty-five years after Mark. Matthew may or may not have been the apostle Matthew.

kingdom of God is the demonstration of power over the kingdom of Satan.[213] Flesh and blood and the unrighteous cannot inherit the kingdom (1 Cor. 6:9; 15:50; Gal. 5:19–21). Paul said that the kingdom of God produces righteousness, peace, and joy in the Holy Spirit (Rom. 17:14).

How Does One Coexist with the Kingdom of God?

Salvation is the only possible way of entering into the kingdom of God. This is simply because our spirit has to be reborn, cleansed of sin. Only Jesus can cause that to occur. Once we have entered this spiritual dimension, we begin a journey toward the goal of becoming pure in our spirit, mature, and changed to conform to Jesus' character. During this journey, Satan will be fighting us, but the Holy Spirit will help us change.

Satan, primarily, is in a spirit world that interacts with our physical world.[214] We are in a physical world that is capable of interacting with the spiritual world. It is not good to turn to Satan's kingdom for aid or assistance of any kind.[215] Our purpose is to do just the opposite by aligning ourselves with God. As indicated earlier, salvation is the beginning phase of that experience. Baptism with the Holy Spirit is the next major milestone or experience. Sanctification and maturing is the last phase.

The Bible's Purpose

The Bible is to be revered as the word of God, but it is not an object to be worshiped. Some people claim that the King James Version, as the Authorized

---

213 The demonstration of power has both the tangible evidence as well as the intangible evidence. Clearly, healings, deliverances, and miracles, may be visible signs, if they are truly from God. However, there are also the signs that may not always be visible to others, such as peace, joy, and righteousness in the Holy Spirit.

214 Understand that in addition to the kingdom of God there is the existing alternative kingdom of Satan, which includes his evil spirits or demons, who are at war with man to prove God is wrong about faith.

215 Not only is this not a good idea, but one who does obtain his "help" is on the path to hell. This kind of activity creates opportunities for Satan's demons by granting them permission to greatly influence or control an individual. If you have been involved with black magic, divination, fortune telling, communicating with the dead, and so on, you must repent and perhaps get deliverance.

Version, is the only true version.[216] But in reality, there are a number of excellent modern translations of the Bible now available that render the ancient texts in easy-to-understand language for the modern reader.

However, a more critical issue than choosing a good translation is knowing how to properly view Scripture. The key question must be answered as to whether or not the Bible is true and trustworthy. Recent research by the Barna Group confirms as of 2006 that most Christians in America believe that the Bible is 100 percent accurate in all of its teachings. That same research indicates that only 12 percent of born-again Christians disagree that the Bible is totally accurate. And it is significant to note that 48 percent of all American adults—including non-Christians—strongly believe that the Bible is totally accurate.[217]

In other words, most followers of Christ hold a high view of Scripture, accepting the Bible as the inspired Word of God, without error, and supremely authoritative. On the other hand, a small minority holds a lower view of Scripture, suggesting that the Bible contains errors and contradictions, and also suggesting that the Bible is not meant to be historically and scientifically accurate. This distinction, more than any other, forms the dividing line between evangelicals and non-evangelicals.

It is dangerous to suggest that the Bible contains error and is not meant to be historically and scientifically accurate. If the Bible cannot be trusted in

---

216 Since the King James Version was first released in 1611, many additional copies of earlier manuscripts have been discovered. There have been a few changes to the different version since then, but the purpose of a translation is to bring the original language into the common language so people can understand what was written. Thus, the New King James Version, published in 1982 by Thomas Nelson, attempts to use words that have more meaning today without changing the intent of the authors. Some people will argue that the Bible, as we know it today, is incorrect or in error because scribes may have made unintentional mistakes when making copies of the Scriptures. For this reason they will reject the Bible as being the Word of God. In rebuttal to this basic assumption, consider the following example. If you had one thousand copies of what were intended to be the same puzzle and you thought that each puzzle had twenty random errors or omissions, and you put them all together, what could you conclude by comparing them? You would find that the probability of identical errors was extremely small, and you would be able to easily see where the mistakes or omissions occurred. But by combining the unmistakable and perfect parts from several puzzles, you would have a copy of the perfect, intended puzzle. Our present-day Bible does not contain numerous errors that have not been accounted for; insignificant scribal errors have been identified. Thus, in faith, you can trust the Bible. However, it must be recognized that its words cannot always be extrapolated out of their context, particularly without the Holy Spirit's guidance, and not when you are an immature Christian.

217 The Barna Group, "The Bible," *TheBarnaGroup.org*, http://www.barna.org/FlexPage.aspx?Page=Topic&TopicID=7 (accessed September 8, 2008).

matters of history and science, how can it be trusted in any other matters? If the biblical writers made mistakes in peripheral matters, how do we know they didn't make mistakes in matters that are central to our faith? Either the Bible is trustworthy, or it isn't. If it contains error, who could say which parts are true and which parts aren't? And if some parts are inspired and other parts are not, again, who could say which are which? In essence, the Bible would then be stripped of its divine authority, and man would become the supreme arbiter of truth. But the bottom line in this issue is this: there is no proof that the Bible contains error; it's an empty argument.

Therefore, we uphold the inerrancy of the biblical autographs (i.e., the original documents), even though none of the autographs still exist as far as we know. And we do not consider as errors the minor scribal glitches that occurred down through the ages as thousands of biblical manuscripts were copied by hand. Many of those manuscripts date back close to the time when the original documents were written. So, we can accept with confidence that the Bible is authentic and reliable.

It can be well established from the Gospels that Jesus had an extremely high view of Scripture. On many occasions, He used a word or phrase—sometimes an obscure one—from Old Testament Scripture to validate His teaching and practice. His most sweeping validation of the intricate accuracy and authority of Scripture made reference to the smallest markings in Hebrew writing: "Do not think that I have come to abolish the Law or the Prophets; I have not come to abolish them but to fulfill them. I tell you the truth, until heaven and earth disappear, not the smallest letter, not the least stroke of a pen, will by any means disappear from the Law until everything is accomplished" (Matt. 5:17–18). And he rebuked the Sadducees for their mishandling of Scripture, saying, "You are in error because you do not know the Scriptures or the power of God" (Matt. 22:29). In Jesus' view, every word of Scripture was important.

Once it is settled that the Bible is God's Word, the next logical step is to read it and apply its teachings to our lives. Reading the Bible, combined with insight from the Holy Spirit, leads us into a relationship with God through Jesus Christ. The Bible does not contain all knowledge, but it contains sufficient information for its intended use.

The biblical writers were inspired by God, but this does not necessarily mean they were in a trance, devoid of all personal information, and that they put down verbatim what God was saying to them.[218] For example, Moses

---

218 God would not trust one man to be responsible for His revelation to man. Thus, there is safety in numbers. In this case, approximately forty authors were involved in creating the sixty-six books that are contained in the Bible. Paul wrote more than any other—thirteen to fourteen books.

is credited with writing the first five books of the Old Testament. How did Moses get the information to write about the Garden? Was he in a trance? Did he dream it? Did he have a vision? It is unlikely that any of these occurred. What Moses learned was passed down by oral history from those before him. In addition, it was not passed down through that many people. The lives of Adam, Methuselah, and Noah overlapped for periods of four to five hundred years yet still spanned almost two thousand years all together. Noah's son Shem was alive for most of Abraham's life, and some think he died after Abraham died. Moses was born only four generations after Jacob. God then inspired Moses to accurately recall and record this information. The telling of the family history was an important part of their identity.

In a similar concept, Jesus told the apostles they would remember their experiences as the Holy Spirit enabled them. (See John 14:26.) Thus, Mathew and John were dependent upon the quickening of their memories by the Holy Spirit. This is why the Bible can only be fully interpreted with the help of the Holy Spirit. (See 1 Corinthians 2:9–15.)

The Old Testament is primarily history. It tells us about man's Fall and the aftermath of it. The writers were limited to recounting their interactions with God, which often involved man's rebellious nature and his failure to follow God's instructions. This was something God was well aware of before He created anything. The New Testament concerns Jesus and the birth of His church.[219] Thus, the New Testament provides the blueprint and framework for church doctrine and practice. However, the New Testament does not replace the need for the Holy Spirit, who brings direction and power in the in carrying out Christ's mission. That is why it is so important to be Spirit-filled and to be led by the Holy Spirit. It is not God's intention for us to merely follow written rules, but rather to know Him intimately and to interact with Him in a personal way.

For this reason, wisdom and truth come from the Holy Spirit, not from our own or even man's collective intellect. Nevertheless, it is very important that one understands that whatever they believe they have heard from God, it will never violate Jesus' character nor will it contradict what He has said through the Gospels.[220]

---

219 Notice that Jesus, more than once sent His "students" out to preach the message about the kingdom of God. This was before they really knew who He was. What did they say that laid it out for the people so that they readily accepted it? (See Luke 9:6.)

220 Thus, you do not kill people in the name of God, nor do you hang or torture people to force your concept of God on them. To do so would not create faith in them. In addition, you are not to kill those who you believe are doing something against God's laws. You should pray for them.

Remember that God desires us to worship Him in spirit and truth (John 4:23). Thus, we need to know ourselves as well as know God. That knowledge only comes from the Holy Spirit. This is why the baptism with the Holy Spirit is so important.

In your choice of a Bible to study, you will discover that there are two types of translation methods. One involves a method called formal equivalence, which attempts a word-for-word translation. The second method is called dynamic equivalence, which means the thought and intents are translated and treated as more important than the grammar and style of the original authors. Sometimes the original language cannot convey the same intent in present English. A paraphrased Bible would be a total dynamic equivalence, while a literal version would be an example of formal equivalence; other versions employ a mixture of the last two types.

The literal translations are the King James Version[221] (1611), New King James Version (1982), Young's Literal Translation (1862), New American Standard Bible (1971), and Revised Standard Version (1952). The Living Bible (1971) and the New Living Translation (2004) are two examples of paraphrased translations. Two examples of versions that attempt to offer readers a balance or combination, using literal translation where the meaning would be clear today and communicating the intent of the passage where the literal translation would not convey the meaning adequately in the twentieth century, are the New International Version (1978) and the New Revised Standard Version (1989). Sometimes you can find a single Bible with several translations side by side. This can be helpful in your study.

WHAT DOES INSPIRATION FROM GOD MEAN?

Although briefly discussed previously, more exploration of the subject in greater depth is needed. It was said by Paul that the Scripture was given by inspiration of God, and it was profitable for doctrine, for reproof, for correction,

---

221 The King James Version is often called the Authorized Bible. It was authorized by King James I, begun in 1604, and published in 1611, by the Church of England. A previous "authorized version" was commissioned by King Henry VIII in approximately 1540. (Other English Bibles pre-dated these.) The 1611 version uses an early modern-English vocabulary and grammar. Over the next 150 years, it underwent four reprints for typos and grammatical and spelling errors. Some people have a mystical reverence for this version, which fails to account for the fact that later versions have the benefit of large amounts of additional reference materials.

for instruction in righteousness. (See 2 Timothy 3:16.)[222] Peter equates Paul's letters, at least those he had read, to Scripture. (See 2 Peter 3:15.)[223] There is some confusion on what is involved when God inspires someone when he is writing a document. A dictionary would probably explain it as a divine influence to receive and communicate sacred revelation. Given this, it would appear strange if an angel appeared and instructed you about what to write. One might understand this to mean that the writer was not sensitive enough for God to inspire. On the other hand, perhaps it only indicates that the writer does not have the capability to take dictation. In either case, it is not inspiration from God to have an angel as the intermediary, since you cannot be sure the angel is actually from God. It could be from Satan, particularly if the angel spoke of new ideas that could not be confirmed by the rest of the Word of God. If it is from God, any new revelation fulfills or expands upon the earlier revelation; it does not contradict it. Angels have been messengers from God for a specific situation. One example was when the angel told Joseph about Mary's situation. However, God does not use angels to deliver his Word. In addition, if the angel claims to offer a new revelation, how could you, hearing for the first time this new revelation, be sure it isn't just a figment of your imagination, or worse, a vision and lie spoken by Satan appearing as an angel? Satan can appear as an angel of light, and thus, alleged new messages delivered by angels should be avoided. Therefore, for any new perspective or understanding to qualify as inspiration from God, it must come directly from God, and it will not directly conflict with previous revelation.

So, how does God communicate? Does the author go into a meditative state? No. Does the author write very fast to keep up with God's dictation? No. The raw materials are already within a person's mind, usually from observations or other human sources, which may or may not have been made available through God's influence. The author may include historical or factual information in his document. An example would be Luke's account of facts concerning the earliest period of the church, which he presented in Acts. The author could also relate personal information, such as greetings. However, at some point the purpose or subject of the document is constructed

---

222   Writing in approximately A.D. 63, Paul was probably referring to the first three Gospels that had been written. It would be confusing if this passage is meant that one should be using the Old Testament laws as a means to instruct and correct Gentiles unless the underlying spiritual principles were explained.

223   Most, if not all, of Paul's letters had been written by that time. However, probably not all had been copied and circulated by the time of Peter's letter.

and conveyed. The inspiration from God lies in what information, within the available information, becomes part of the final content, as well as the way it is expressed. However, the author's method of literary expression is controlled by the author. His personality comes through.[224] In Paul's case, he gave advice that was sometimes predicated upon an imminent return of Jesus. The inspiration from God is revealed in the document's contents, and since the Holy Spirit is leading the author, He reveals its true meaning to us. It is only the Holy Spirit who can explain all parts of the Scriptures, particularly the interdependence of what is expressed. We should read the Bible many times to gather as much understanding as we can, remain open, and expect the Holy Spirit to give additional insight when He considers it necessary.

There are two basic schools of thought regarding biblical inspiration. Some argue that the Bible, both Old and New Testaments, are completely the inspired Word of God. They say that it is exactly as God wants it to be,[225] meaning that every word is exactly as God wanted it to be, at least as it was originally written. There is another position that should be considered in your understanding of the meaning of *inspiration*. These individuals believe that it is only the ideas and revelation that are inspired and that it isn't necessarily every exact word and their sequence.[226]

The apostles and other believers did a lot of writing in the early years of the church, and not every document written by a particular author was later considered to be inspired by God. That was a judgment that was sometimes made several hundred years later. The original writings are called "autographs." It is believed that none exist, but then again we have nothing that is a proven sample of a particular author or scribe. Because of the importance of the writings, they were rapidly copied and circulated. During the first one to two hundred years of the faith, several of the early church fathers quoted

---

224 Note how the Gospels are different and even how Paul's letters, if read in chronological order, change over time.

225 The Bible is the primary means through which we acquire information about God. Any supplemental information we acquire will not conflict with a proper understanding of the Bible as revealed by the Holy Spirit. It is the standard we measure against for any claim of new revelation. In this process, the factual context contained within the writings should not be ignored.

226 Usually someone else will have to make the determination on the true source of the inspiration. If the author makes the statement that, he is writing the Word of God, one should be immediately on guard because the author could be saying this in order to manipulate the reader, or give himself credibility. The issue becomes; do you trust the messenger? If it is from God, and if you are a Christian, your spirit will bear *complete* witness to it, if only a partial acceptance, then it should be rejected until otherwise confirmed by the Holy Spirit. God never drives us into anything new, it is progressive and at our own speed.

extensively from the various letters and books. Sometimes they cited two thousand quotations from almost every book that would later be compiled into a single volume, the New Testament, approximately three hundred years after Jesus died. Thus, the originals have been extensively confirmed from several different sources over several hundred years. It was not until after the Gutenberg Bible was published in 1454 that a printing press made it possible to quickly produce multiple copies of the Scriptures. But, prior to that event there were over five thousand handmade copies of at least part of the New Testament, which still exist, and over 50,000 quotations from various parts of the New Testament made by the Church Fathers. Many of these, especially those written by such individuals as Ignatius (30–107), Polycarp (65–155), Papias (70–155), Clement of Rome (approximately 60–101), Justin Martyr (110–165), Clement of Alexandria (193–220), and Cyprian (200–258), still exist.[227]

In the final analysis, it makes little difference who is correct about what inspiration from God means, because the basic Christian principles are generally agreed upon by both approaches. The Holy Spirit reveals to us what the inspiration really is, and it is not based upon an intellectual exercise. Thus, the Bible is the Word of God, inspired by God, and revealed by God to us. Since we are in the Era of Faith, all revelation should be questioned to determine if it increases our faith in Jesus. Does it conflict with the New Testament? Does it conflict with what Jesus said about Himself, the Father, and the Holy Spirit? If so, it should not be accepted.

Is Homosexuality Permissible for Christians?

It is clear that in the Old Testament, particularly Genesis and in the laws that God gave the Israelites, homosexuality was forbidden, with punishment by death (Lev. 20:13–16). (Other offenses that resulted in the death penalty were human sacrifice [Lev. 20:2], blaspheming the Lord [Lev. 24:11, 16], rape [Deut. 22:24], and murder [Deut. 21:22].) Later, in the New Testament, Paul, Jude, and Peter spoke against homosexuality as well as other sexual sins.[228] In fact, Paul said you cannot inherent the kingdom of God while practicing homosexuality.

---

227 See *Adam Clarke's Commentary on the New Testament*; *Jamieson, Fausset, and Brown's Commentary on the Whole Bible*; and en.Wikipedia.org/wiki/church_fathers (accessed September 26, 2008).

228 Peter was more general in that he stated that people should not fall back to the evil desires they once had when ignorant about Jesus (2 Pet. 3:17). Peter was ministering to the Jews. Thus, he would have no reason to mention sexual immorality because that was already prohibited by their culture, society, and Jewish laws.

(See 1 Corinthians 6:9.) The real issue is that people who engage in homosexual acts should know the consequences. Some religions deal harshly with homosexual acts. Christianity does not punish people under a religious legal system, however, since homosexuality is a lifestyle of sin, it will prevent you from fellowshiping with Jesus.

There are several arguments being made excusing homosexuality. First, there are those that point out that Jesus did not speak against it; second, that Jesus wants all and welcomes all people; third, that very little is said about being gay, and only certain sexual acts in the wrong place and at the wrong time are prohibited; fourth, that sometimes it is a matter of the genes, such that homosexuals cannot help themselves; fifth, that the Bible does not say homosexuality is a sin; sixth, that John 3:16 says that whoever believes in Him will be saved (regardless of sexual preference); seventh, that the Genesis 19 account dealt with rape, not homosexuality; eighth, that Leviticus 18:22 and 20:13 only dealt with temple prostitutes; and ninth, that some close relationships recorded in the Scriptures, such as those between David and Jonathan, and Ruth and Naomi, may have had sexual conduct. The list could probably include several other arguments, but the extent and scope is illustrated.

My responses to these arguments are as follows.

"Jesus did not speak against it."

The argument has been made that Jesus did not mention it. However, we really do not know that for a fact because not everything He said is recorded. Jesus ministered for two or three years, so not all of His teachings could be recorded in the Gospels. If you were to read the red-letter parts of the Gospels without repeating the same accounts over again in the different Gospel versions, it would take less than one day to read. Clearly, Jesus had a lot more to say during the span of His ministry, but the most important messages are included in the canon. Perhaps Jesus' teaching on homosexuality, if He did teach on it, was not included in the canon because homosexuality was already prohibited in the Old Testament Scriptures. Was He supposed to repeat it? Were Jesus and the Gospel writers under the obligation to recount or restate all of the sins and all the acts of man that hinder God's plan of salvation?

When the Gospels were written, it was necessary for the Holy Spirit to bring back to the remembrance of the witnesses the important and necessary words of Jesus.[229] Homosexuality, as well as other major sins that were punishable by

---

229 Mark, a disciple and later an assistant to Peter, is credited with the first written Gospel. The Gospel of Mark, relying on Peter's input. The Gospel writer Luke, who traveled with Paul in the latter years of his ministry, came well after Jesus died.

death, are not mentioned in the Gospels. In fact, if you read carefully you will notice that Jesus did not teach specifically about many of the spiritual sins; He would just group them together.[230] When He did single one out, as when He was speaking about adultery, He said, "Do not lust" (Matt. 5:28, author's paraphrase). He was addressing the root problem, lust within the heart or spirit. Thus, He was talking about changing from a system of prohibited acts to a Spirit-based system. He dealt with hypocrisy, mercy, forgiveness, and love. All of these things relate to your spirit. Naturally, He did not waste time talking about prohibited acts. The point to remember was that Jesus said He came to fulfill the Law, that is, to elevate it to the level of spiritual principles that could be assimilated into our hearts.

"Jesus wants all and welcomes all people, including homosexuals. Very little is said in the Scriptures about being gay, and only certain sexual acts in the wrong place and at the wrong time are prohibited."

Yes, Jesus wants all to come to Him by believing in Him. However, that is merely the beginning. He does not want you to remain ignorant and continue in sin. Jesus' invitation is not a "come as you are and stay that way" type of call. First, there is salvation, then there is the journey on the narrow path. There do not appear to be special instances or situations where homosexuality and other types of sexual immorality are allowed. Sexual immorality is either sin, or it is not. Sexual relationships that do not enhance the spiritual bonding between a man and woman as husband and wife merely gratify the flesh. Gratifying the flesh is something we should attempt to avoid because we should live by the spirit. (See Romans 8:4; 1 Peter 4:6; and 1 John 4:13.)

The importance of the spiritual bonding that is possible with a married man and woman cannot be dismissed. It is a foretaste of the relationship of your spirit with Jesus', in which there is trust, love, and oneness with God. Thus, outsiders should not break that bond. Homosexuality dismisses God's plan for the spiritual bonding that is possible through Jesus.

---

230 In Mark 7:20–23, Jesus gave several examples of sins of the spirit, "It is what comes out of a person that makes a person unclean. For it is from within, from the human heart, that evil thoughts come, as well as sexual immorality, stealing, murder, adultery, greed, wickedness, cheating, shameless lust, envy, slander, arrogance, and foolishness. All these things come from within and make a person unclean" (isv). Undoubtedly, there are different acts that can be identified under the same descriptor of sexual immorality.

"Sometimes homosexuality is a matter of the genes, and those who are affected by it cannot help whom they are attracted to."

Another current theory is that homosexuals cannot help themselves because sexual orientation is controlled by the genes. If homosexuality were controlled by the genes, and God prohibits that lifestyle, then that would mean God was being unfair and unjust. Some might even, in that case, try to argue that God was wrong when He destroyed Sodom and Gomorrah. Furthermore, some might say that the genes have mutated since then, such that homosexuality was not a genetic problem during that time period, as it is now. God, however, did not limit the prohibition against homosexuality to a set period of time, after which it would be permissible. This is further indication that nothing, genetically or otherwise, has changed.

In the case of those who some claim are rendered homosexual by birth defects (such as hermaphrodism) or whose reproductive organs are damaged by some accidental occurrence, celibacy is the answer unless God intervenes. In addition, if someone wanted to make an exception for those with imperfect genes, is there a test that can prove that homosexuality is caused by a particular mutation of a particular gene? No, there is no proof. However, there does not need to be because it may not be the genes, but instead a spirit.

If homosexuality is okay, then everyone should be able to do it. The problem is, if they did, the human race would cease to exist in fifty to seventy-five years. Thus, God's plans would be blocked. Who would have the most to gain in that event? Satan. Clearly, homosexuality would not be a good thing.

The reason Paul was adamant concerning sexual immorality and other sins was the continual nature of the sin, which forms a lifestyle (Rom. 1:24–25). Thus, in time, the lifestyle of sin makes a person insensitive and reprobate, when the body is supposed to be the temple of the Holy Spirit (1 Cor. 3:16). *Reprobate* means that you can no longer distinguish other sins and the Holy Spirit's prompting is rejected. Almost universally, homosexuality is a matter of choice, at least initially. It can be difficult to give up the desire if a spirit of homosexuality has entered and influences or controls that desire. It is difficult to cast out, but it can be done. The point is, however, do not allow yourself to come under a demon's control on any level. The homosexual spirit is merely one of the ones that outwardly affect a person's inclinations and emotions.[231]

"The Bible does not say homosexuality is a sin."

Granted, the exact words "homosexuality is sin" are not in the Bible. However, in Leviticus 18:22, a man lying with another man like a woman is called "detestable" (NIV) or "an abomination" (ASV, DNT, KJV, NKJV, and YLT). In 1 Timothy 1:9–11 (ISV), Paul includes homosexuals as part of a group of ungodly people and sinners. The Revised Standard Version and New King James Version include fornicators and sodomites in this group. Thus, the words may be different but the meaning is there.

"John 3:16 says that whoever believes in Him will be saved."

Yes, John 3:16 says to believe in Jesus and be saved. However, is that all we must do? Can you then still live a life of sin and never change anything? Paul said the wicked would not inherit the kingdom of God (1 Cor. 6:9, ISV, NKJV). He included male prostitutes and homosexual offenders. You cannot continue living as a wicked person, because if you do, it is like crucifying Jesus again with your unrepentant sin. Paul said you must rid yourself of these sins (Col. 3:5–10).

"The Genesis 19 account dealt with rape. Leviticus 18:22 and 20:13 only dealt with temple prostitutes. In addition, some close relationships, such as those between David and Jonathan, and Ruth and Naomi may have involved sexual conduct."

Contrary to the argument that Sodom and Gomorrah were destroyed because the men of the city tried to rape the angels that were visiting Lot's family, the angels' account, described in Genesis 19, was just the final straw. The planned destruction had already been set in motion before the incident with the angels occurred. (See Genesis 18.)

Homosexual temple prostitutes are, indeed, mentioned in some translations of Deuteronomy 23:17–18. (The King James Version uses the term *sodomites*; the New King James Version uses the phrase *perverted one*.) However, after over fifteen prohibitions elsewhere in the Law regarding sexual relations,

---

231 Normally, negative emotions that cause an individual to react rather than respond reasonably to situations are most likely caused by spirits. Demonic spirits can influence everyone, usually from outside us but sometimes from within us. They cannot possess a Christian because the Spirit of Jesus is within us. Most of the time, negative emotions are merely due to flesh patterns we have developed during our life. However, if we are unable to change after seeking the Lord's help, then it may be because of a spirit's influence. If a person, after being saved by Jesus, cannot change through prayer, then more help needs to be sought from a pastor to see if deliverance is required.

Leviticus 18:22 clearly says a man shall not lie with a man like he would lie with a woman (KJV, NKJV, NIV, YLT, NRSV, DNT, and ASV). These seven translations do not mention that the prohibition only applied to temple prostitutes.

The Bible does not say that the relationship between David and Jonathan, and Ruth and Naomi had a sexual component, either. Regarding David and Jonathan, while David's statement in 2 Samuel 1:26 is poetic, it does not mean that the relationship was sexual in any way. Many people today, in their attempt to defend homosexuality as an acceptable lifestyle, point out that the terms used in the Bible's restrictions may not refer to what we understand to be homosexual behavior today. They would seek exhaustive and, as a result, explicit explanations of sex acts from the Scriptures instead of conceding simply that the Bible calls homosexual activity a sin.

What did the New Testament writer Paul say about it? Paul briefly recounts a time when men in the early days, although they knew about God, still carried on with idol worship, sexual impurity, and so on. He gives two examples, one in which females exchanged natural relations for unnatural relations and men exchanged relations with women for sexual relations with other men (Rom. 1:26–27). God's wrath came upon them. Paul continues, however, and instructs people to behave decently, avoiding many things, including sexual immorality (Rom. 13:13). He points out that the body is not meant for sexual immorality (1 Cor. 6:13). We are to flee from it (1 Cor. 6:18). Paul also said to live by the spirit, which will not gratify the desires of the sinful nature, and lists sexual immorality among other types of "sinful acts" (Gal. 5:16–19). (See also Ephesians 5:3; Colossians 3:5; and 1 Thessalonians 4:3.)

Paul said clearly, "Do you not know that the wicked will not inherit the kingdom of God? Do not be deceived: Neither the sexually immoral nor idolaters nor adulterers nor male prostitutes nor homosexual offenders nor thieves nor the greedy nor drunkards nor slanderers nor swindlers will inherit the kingdom of God" (1 Cor. 6:9–10). Again, in Ephesians 5:5–6, he said, "For of this you can be sure: No immoral, impure or greedy person—such a man is an idolater—has any inheritance in the kingdom of Christ and of God. Let no one deceive you with empty words, for because of such things God's wrath comes on those who are disobedient."

Jude is another New Testament writer to speak against homosexual acts that occurred in Sodom and Gomorrah (Jude 1:7, TLB). Also, one cannot ignore John's statement in Revelation 21:8 that the sexually immoral, as well as others, will burn in the lake burning with fire and brimstone, the second death.

In conclusion, it is clear that if you want to look for something to exempt homosexuality from a list of prohibited acts—and you are willing to tailor your analysis and interpretation of the Scriptures to get the "results" you want—you can probably succeed in your efforts at proof-texting.[232] However, at what cost is the Word of God subverted? Remember, it is the condition of your spirit that is at issue. You subvert truth when you try to excuse your actions by manipulating the Bible to justify sin. You do yourself grave harm.

WHAT IS THE CHURCH'S MISSION?

The church is not a particular denomination or religious institution. It is like the kingdom of God; it has no physical parameters. It is an unofficial organization, without appointed leaders or structure, but with Jesus as its Head. Thus, it is composed of individuals in combination and in unity, where the sum is greater than the parts. It will be the bride of Christ.

Nonetheless, the church's mission is not simple. It is to make all nations disciples of Jesus by spreading the truth about Jesus and salvation through Him, and guiding people through the sanctification process, which includes several stages of maturation (Matt. 28:18). This has at least one purpose: to bring us into unity. Jesus said,

> Sanctify them by Your truth. Your word is truth. As You sent Me into the world, I also have sent them into the world. And for their sakes I sanctify Myself, that they also may be sanctified by the truth. I do not pray for these alone, but also for those who will believe in Me through their word; that they all may be one, as You, Father, are in Me, and I in You; that they also may be one in Us, that the world may believe that You sent Me. And the glory which You gave Me I have given them, that they may be one just as We are one: I in them, and You in Me; that they may be made perfect in one ["brought to complete unity," NIV], and that the world may know that You have sent Me, and have loved them as You have loved Me. Father, I desire that they also whom You gave Me may be with Me where I am, that they may behold My glory which You have given Me; for You loved Me before the foundation of the world. O righteous Father! The world has not known You, but I have known You; and these have known that You sent Me. And I have declared to them Your name, and will declare it, that the love with which You loved Me may be in them, and I in them.
>
> —JOHN 17:17–26, NKJV

---

232   Proof-texting is a method where you focus only upon those scriptures that support your premise, to the exclusion of anything that would conflict with or not support your premise. This is a common practice that is employed when new "revelations" are discovered. The study of the Bible should be an evolving progress, not a process used to merely prove your existing argument or position.

It would appear, then, that the church should focus on the underlying beliefs that bring us into unity.

Some Christian denominations often distinguish themselves by the controls they place on their members. These cause the members to deceive themselves concerning their righteousness. For example, the restriction of certain musical instruments in services, sports on Sunday, drinking alcohol in any amounts—the fact that Jesus drank a wine seems to be ignored—gambling, and other banned "negative" activities, makes the outer man appear to be righteous. They are, in effect, grooming hypocrites, which seems a somewhat strange purpose for a local church considering Jesus' condemnation of hypocrites. Control of the flesh does not instill or create a righteous spirit. It is only a righteous spirit that counts with God.

Church organizations promote control of the flesh as desirable because it is easier to evaluate than a person's spiritual maturation. Along this vein is the idea of tithing. It is a complicated Old Testament concept not directly applicable in today's economic system, where few of us are farmers. Abraham gave 10 percent of the spoils of battle, but we seldom acquire wealth in that manner. The church finds it easier to urge members to tithe because it is easier to plan and maintain an infrastructure of buildings and staff. However, in doing so, it ignores the fact that God wants a cheerful giver, in other words, someone who is not reluctant, angry, bitter, or under a compulsion to give money to a local church. Perhaps for this reason, Paul does not say anything about tithing. Some may argue that tithing was expected, so Paul did not mention it. However, this is a legalistic interpretation and misses the point that we are, since Christ, in an era of faith (Rom. 3:28; Gal. 2:16; Phil. 3:9). Instead, Paul wrote about being led by the Spirit in 2 Corinthians 9:7. He explained that gifts to the church were not to be under compulsion or out of proportion. Thus, the gift was not based upon a fixed rate, head tax, or other externally mandated amount.

Without financial support, the church could not exist. Monetary contributions should be a balance of placing Jesus first, then your family's needs, and then the joy you experience. If it is done out of obligation, it is not from the Holy Spirit. In times of special financial need, you should listen to the Holy Spirit's guidance.

When Jesus mentioned tithing, He was speaking to those still under the Law. He condemned their use of the act of tithing as the primary criteria for a person to feel approved by God or for the religious leaders to esteem and grant favors to people based upon their financial support. The fact that tithing is not written about by the New Testament authors may indicate that they recognized that it does not require faith to perform and can be a source of pride and/or resentment.

The early church leaders did not mention tithing as part of the rules they gave the Gentiles to follow. Recognize that for a number of years, Christianity was considered a sect of the Jewish faith, and there was some struggle to discern how to mix their cultural traditions with Jesus' teachings about salvation, particularly for the Gentile (Acts 21:25). They had mixed feelings about the Gentiles' relationship to the Jewish Law,[233] because for the first nineteen to twenty years after the Ascension, nothing had been written down and copied for others to read. Thus, the early ministry was based upon oral teachings, and it was not until Paul began writing that the Era of Faith became understood. This was particularly explained in his letter to the Romans.[234]

Now, however, in this era of faith, the church must fully understand that the Law was merely dealing with the activities of people's flesh. It did not directly address the spirit or heart of a person. The change of a person's spirit is only brought about by the relationship a person has with God throughout life, a relationship based upon faith in our walk with God.

Thus, the primary mission of the church is to make disciples of all nations by spreading the gospel of Jesus and helping to prepare us to understand God, who we are, and how our relationship with Jesus is meant to change us into His likeness. This is not a simple task. It does not involve creating rules of conduct, but instead the church should deal with the sanctification of the spirit.

A second mission of the church is to help believers mature. Thus, the church must recognize that Satan is at war with the church as well as with its members. One of the primary attacks by Satan on the local church is through religious spirits in people. These people often seem highly motivated, however, in reality

---

233 This lasted for perhaps two hundred years. However, by A.D. 300 there became a clear separation in doctrine and practice between the Jews and the Christian Jews. The separation was caused by several factors, one of which was the fact that the world did not end as the Jewish Christians thought Jesus had promised. Thus, they rejected Him as the Messiah and persecuted the early Christians for their beliefs. (See en.Wikipedia.org/wiki/persecution_of_Christians, accessed September 26, 2008.)

234 Paul's letter to the Romans was written approximately twenty years after his conversion. The earliest letter he wrote that we have a copy of was written about fourteen years after his conversion and the last about twenty-eight years afterwards. Paul may have written earlier letters but they were either lost or were not later on considered inspired by God for inclusion in the Canon.

they are people seeking God's approval.[235] It is tragic when a leader of a local church has a religious spirit.

Some characteristics of a religious spirit include:

- When an individual believes him or herself to be spiritually superior to others. Often they take on the role of judging other ministries in the body of Christ. They can even believe they have a calling to "protect" the faith.
- Religious pride—Some may act as though they are full of their own self-importance, as if they are better than others.
- When an individual espouses dogma that places others in bondage, either to themselves or to a theory of salvation by good works.
- When an individual considers positional authority—such as church leadership, headship of a local organization or of a large church—as being equal to approval from God and/or as having a special favor with God. They will also confuse success by man's standards as approval and authority from God. (In fact, approval from large groups of people is often a danger sign.) (See 2 Corinthians 10:18; 1 Thessalonians 2:4.)

The influence and effects of demons on humanity has not disappeared since Jesus came two thousand years ago. They generally have to be invited into us or at least be given tacit permission to enter us. Often this permission is given by indulging in certain sinful activities or negative emotions. Regardless, you can be set free through deliverance. In addition, if spiritually mature enough, you can pray deliverance over yourself and receive it through the power of the Holy Spirit. Demons can tell when you know your authority is from God (Acts 19:13–15).

There is a class of demons that affect emotional and behavior patterns within us. Examples of these are lust, greed, fear, and anger. Others have a greater impact, such as homosexuality. This spirit becomes so attached that it controls the sexuality of a person. Thus, it affects one of man's strongest drives. How can you tell if a spirit is responsible for your behavior? Spirits drive and compel a person into a negative pattern of behavior they cannot stop by willpower or

---

235 Religious spirits can drive a person to fervently perform religious acts or to pursue religious causes. These acts mask the true condition of a person's spirit. Pride is often coupled with this spirit, as the individual believes he or she is special and has God's approval. In order to receive God's grace, one cannot be proud, particularly because of religious activities.

even after prayer. They cause a person to react rather than respond to a situation. A reaction is almost instantaneous, while the other is more measured.

Fortunately for Christians, spirits cannot possess you because of the presence of the Spirit of Jesus. However, they can occupy areas within us. The sanctification process involves the cleansing of our spirit from these demonic influences. For example, strong emotions such as hate, guilt, fear, and anger may be caused by a spirit that we unknowingly allowed into us, probably before being saved. This is evident with any evoked emotion that is consistently expressed as a reaction rather than a response. These spirits cannot be removed by merely using external means, but only by the working of the Holy Spirit in conjunction with our own spirit. Obeying laws or chastising ourselves will not deal with the problem with our spirit. That is one reason why the Law is not sufficient. It merely makes our outer man appear to others or even ourselves as being righteous. Thus, we become hypocrites. In religious activities, we can even become self-righteous because of our "good" works. Those actions come from the flesh and are motivated by fleshly desires, but spiritual works have the right motives, such as love, compassion, and mercy. However, salvation and the sanctification process are not achieved by our good works.

IS THERE A PERFECT SIZE FOR A CHURCH?

Originally, the local, early Christian churches sometimes met in synagogues on Sundays, though in most cases they met in homes. (See Acts 2:46; 5:42.) At that time, Christianity was still considered a Jewish sect. Understand, however, that from a structural perspective, houses did not have a very large floor span, except in the upper room, the floor of which was supported by columns from the ground floor. The roof was very light, perhaps made from straw or similar materials. Therefore, there was the problem that structures with roofs could not hold very many people. In addition, the distance of travel would limit the area from which people would come to a particular church because most people had to walk. The early Christians were accustomed to having synagogues no farther than three-quarters of a mile away from population centers since on the Sabbath believers were to limit their physical activity.

For these reasons, churches tended to be small and the church members were closely knit. The congregations started small and they were independent, without any affiliation to a greater organization. Later on, an organizational structure was added, and usually covered a larger town or city. Bishops or elders, who oversaw the smaller, individual churches, were installed to provide more church government. They provided guidance and helped to resolve disputes and make judgments regarding sinful activities. This became particularly important when the church moved into the Gentile world, which did not have the background of the Jewish society's standards for acceptable conduct. In other words, because the Gentiles did not have God's Law in their upbringing, they tended to be extremely sinful. In particular, what was to them relatively common sexual behavior was unthinkable in the Jewish culture and punishable by stoning and death according to Jewish Law.

Just because churches started small does not mean that small churches have any special status. It is true that smaller congregations often develop a strong sense of community, which is good. There is also the potential for control issues to emerge. In other words, it becomes possible for the members of leadership to forget their humble beginnings, forget that they are meant to be a servant, and allow their "elevated" position over a close community to lead to some tragic results. On the other hand, when they are independent, small churches can become legalistic in their control over the members. Some modern pharisaic churches, particularly those who believe in a mental rather than spiritual approach to biblical interpretation, use selected verses to manipulate their members' behavior and shun or excommunicate congregants as a means of control. They misunderstand the context of Paul's teachings and fail to distinguish between his short-term or church-specific teachings and those that have a more general application. However, worse than these problems is the likelihood that religious spirits may take over control of or strongly influence the church leadership and members. Thus, when considering a small church today, one should be careful of three potential problems: limited spiritual growth potential, religious spirits in church leadership, or problems with some individuals seeking control.

On the other end of the spectrum, there are the mega-churches. At these churches, it is often difficult to obtain a sense of community unless you joined when the church congregation numbered between two and three hundred people and was still growing. One should determine why the church is so large. What made it grow? Is the minister merely preaching a message that the congregation wants to hear, or is he or she preaching the truth? Is the service filled with entertainment? These churches also have potential problems, including the same control issues, religious spirits, and legalistic issues. Mega-churches and their buildings tend to become a monument to the founder, and many preach and expect tithing and promise material blessings from God because of one's obedience. Too often these large churches—which are housed in large buildings—place equally large financial obligations on the members in order to stay open.

A potential problem of large churches that does not exist with the smaller church is the tendency to equate the size and number of members with approval from God. Some reason that only God would make a church grow, if a church is large, the leaders must be doing God's will. However, the sheep are usually not qualified to pass judgment on the quality of the shepherd. Clearly, Satan may also influence the growth of a church, particularly if the church's message focuses upon the ego of the pastor or congregation. If the music is merely entertaining and the message makes the members feel good about themselves, Satan may tempt individuals to believe that they are better than other Christians. Thus, the size of the membership is a potentially dangerous standard to use in making a determination about the local church you want to attend.

In addition to the size of a church, denominational affiliation is also something many people take into consideration. In my experience, attending an independent church is neither a plus or minus. Denominations do not automatically provide safety, but there is at least some structure overseeing the local church. In an independent church, there is no check-and-balance system ensuring that the leaders' actions are controlled by God, not their own egos.

Of course, there are exceptions to the problem areas I have mentioned for both small and extremely large churches. When one is evaluating a church, he or she should discern if the leader is saved, knows Jesus, has a humble spirit, and finally, if he or she feels a confirmation in their spirit about the situation. In this case, "feelings" is an inadequate expression. What you want is sensitivity to the Holy Spirit and a sense of confirmation in your spirit. Remember that once you join a church, it does not mean you are there for life. No matter how long you have been a part of a congregation, you still have to be sensitive to the Holy Spirit and listen to hear how long you are to remain there. If the church leadership no longer reflects the character of God, seek direction from the Holy Spirit and determine whether or not it is time to move on. In other words, once you join, you are responsible for judging when and if you are to leave.

WILL GOD STRIKE DOWN FALSE PROPHETS?

What is a prophet? According to Merriam-Webster's Dictionary, the word *prophet* has several definitions:

1. one who utters divinely inspired revelations;
2. one gifted with more than ordinary spiritual and moral insight;
3. one who foretells future events; and
4. an effective or leading spokesman for a cause, doctrine, or group.

We usually think of the first definition. In other words, a prophet is perceived as someone who stands in a pulpit speaking about things relating to God, but in a way that is different from the teachings of a teacher or a pastor. However, the prophet and teacher can be similar.

What did Jesus say?

> Watch out for false prophets. They come to you in sheep's clothing, but inwardly they are ferocious wolves. By their fruit you will recognize them. Do people pick grapes from thornbushes, or figs from thistles? Likewise every good tree bears good fruit, but a bad tree bears bad fruit. A good tree cannot bear bad fruit, and a bad tree cannot bear good fruit. Every tree that does not bear good fruit is cut down and thrown into the fire. Thus, by their fruit you will recognize them.
>
> —MATTHEW 7:15–20

> For false Christs and false prophets will appear and perform great signs and miracles to deceive even the elect—if that were possible.
>
> —MATTHEW 24:24

The apostle Peter wrote in 2 Peter 2:1–3:

> But there were also false prophets among the people, just as there will be false teachers among you. They will secretly introduce destructive heresies, even denying the sovereign Lord who bought them—bringing swift destruction on themselves. Many will follow their shameful ways and will bring the way of truth into disrepute. In their greed these teachers will exploit you with stories they have made up. Their condemnation has long been hanging over them, and their destruction has not been sleeping.

The apostle John wrote in 1 John 4:1–3:

> Dear friends, do not believe every spirit, but test the spirits to see whether they are from God, because many false prophets have gone out into the world. This is how you can recognize the Spirit of God: Every spirit that acknowledges that Jesus Christ has come in the flesh is from God, but every spirit that does not acknowledge Jesus is not from God. This is the spirit of the antichrist, which you have heard is coming and even now is already in the world.

Does God kill false prophets? No. He did not in Paul's time, and He does not now. False prophets will come, but we are called to discern or judge their message and compare it with the Word and Spirit of God. He will not always remove them because they can be a means of maturation for believers. God allows people—even false prophets—to exercise their free will without His intervention. People sometimes assume that if God does not strike a prophet down in a dramatic way, he or she must not be heretical. (However, if they died in a "natural" way, people would probably still find some reason to believe that it was not God removing them for being false prophets.) Imagine if God did strike people down for teaching falsely about Him. How bad would someone have to be before He struck him or her down? Would prophets be allowed any mistakes, or would he or she have to be perfect? If this were the way God operated, no one would want to be a prophet!

Today there are false doctrines that have been around for fifty years, 150 years, and some for nearly 1,900 years. In fact, even before Jesus came, Satan was preparing the groundwork for this deception. After Jesus died, Satan immediately found people, often those with religious spirits, and got them to start to question basic concepts, such as the Resurrection. Though Satan has been defeated, he still has this opportunity because it is not yet time for his final judgment. That is why after nearly two thousand years the idea is still around that Jesus was just a man without any divine existence prior to the Incarnation.

Remember that after salvation the path is narrow, meaning that truth must be sought out. It is easy to veer off the true path into false doctrine. What may seem like truth to the mind of reason is often merely the doctrine of man, or worse, Satan.

Is There Really a Hell?

Whether hell exists should not really be questioned because Jesus said it did. Regardless of the term or language used to refer to it, we may be certain from the Scriptures that it is a place where people remain for all of their existence separated from God.

Hell is sometimes equated with a place referred to as *Hades* (New Testament) and *Sheol* (Old Testament), but each of these terms refers to a place of departed spirits where the dead congregated before Jesus died. (Since Jesus came, the saints are immediately with the Lord after the death of their bodies [2 Cor. 5:8].) The valley of Hinnom, called *Gehenna* in Greek, is the place where rubbish was gathered and burned. It is from the name of that place that the New Testament word for *hell* is derived.

Most Bible translations of the New Testament use the term *hell*. All four Gospels state that Jesus used the term (Matt. 5:22, 29; 10:28; 18:9; 23:33). Jesus said people could be cast down to hell, where there is fire (Luke 12:5; Mark 9:47). John used the equivalent by quoting Jesus as saying those who do not abide in Him are gathered and thrown into the fire (John 15:6). James and Peter were the only non-Gospel writers to use the term (James 3:6; 2 Pet. 2:4).

Sometimes Jesus did not use the word *hell*, however in each of these instances He described the attributes of hell. For example, in Matthew 25:41, 46 (NKJV), He said, "Then He will also say to those on the left hand, 'Depart from Me, you cursed, into the everlasting fire prepared for the devil and his angels'....And these will go away into everlasting punishment, but the righteous into eternal life." John used the Greek term *Hades* in the Book of Revelation to refer to this place (Rev. 1:18; 6:8; 20:13–14). Paul said in 2 Thessalonians 1:9, that there was an everlasting destruction in store for those who do not know God and do not obey the gospel of our Lord Jesus: "They will be punished with everlasting destruction and shut out from the presence of the Lord and from the majesty of his power."

Even though Paul is clear about hell, some people believe that it is only a temporary place where people will have a second chance to believe in Jesus. This grants nonbelievers the opportunity to practice their own beliefs now, but later on, after death, they get a second chance to get it right. To justify this belief, they take a verse of scripture and mistakenly apply it to fit their doctrine. For example, in Romans 5:18–19, Paul says that Jesus died for all men. From this statement, they argue that all men are saved because of Jesus' sacrifice. What they will ignore is the fact that salvation is conditional upon an individual's belief that Jesus died for his or her sin and a willing surrender of pride in order to ask Him into their heart. Jesus said, "For my Father's will is that everyone who looks to the Son and believes in him shall have eternal life, and I will raise him up at the last day" (John 6:40). If that is unclear, consider what Jesus said in John 3:15–16 (NKJV): "Whoever believes in Him should not perish but have eternal life. For God so loved the world that He gave His only begotten Son, that whoever believes in Him should not perish but have everlasting life."

Clearly, Jesus said you have to believe in Him. It is not automatic that since Jesus' resurrection all people are saved. There would not have to be much faith involved in our salvation if, after death, we could stand looking at a resurrected Jesus and then decide to believe in Him. On the other hand, perhaps those that argue this position believe they will be standing around in some interim place in front of two gates, one marked heaven and the other hell, and that they will have the option which gate they want to go through.

Several times Jesus used the term *fire* when speaking about hell (Matt. 5:22; 18:9; Mark 9:43). Satan will be in hell (2 Pet. 2:4; Rev. 20:10). To conclude that there is no hell is based upon a mistaken belief that God will give everyone a second opportunity to accept Jesus as Savior. Those who believe there will be a second chance, after death, for individuals to recognize Jesus and to believe that He is the Son of God ignore the requirement for faith: faith does not come from seeing; seeing comes from faith. Their position is similar to that of dispensationalists.

By Jesus' descriptions, hell, regardless of how an individual interprets the Scriptures, is still a place of separation from God for all eternity. The nature of any change to our spirit upon death is unclear in the Bible. Some of our identity is retained because we apparently are able to recognize people (Luke 16:23). Paul said while we are alive we need to sanctify ourselves.

> It is God's will that you should be sanctified: that you should avoid sexual immorality; that each of you should learn to control his own body in a way that is holy and honorable, not in passionate lust like the heathen, who do not know God; and that in this matter no one should wrong his brother or take advantage of him. The Lord will punish men for all such sins, as we have already told you and warned you. For God did not call us to be impure, but to live a holy life. Therefore, he who rejects this instruction does not reject man but God, who gives you his Holy Spirit.
>
> —1 THESSALONIANS 4:3–8

Thus, not only is evil separated from God's presence, but also we have an obligation to experience the sanctification process so that our spirit will be righteous.

WHY DID JESUS APPEAR TO BE A REBEL TO RELIGIOUS AUTHORITY?

Upon reading the Gospels you will probably wonder why the Jewish religious leaders wanted to kill Jesus since it is clear that they were expecting a messiah, although the exact details of how he would come were disputed among them.

There are numerous Old Testament prophesies about the Messiah.[236] However, the most important purpose of the Messiah doesn't appear to be indicated. Namely, as the ultimate and final blood sacrifice for Man's sin.

When John wrote his Gospel many years after the Old Testament books were written, he quoted John the Baptist as identifying Jesus as the Lamb of God (John 1:29, 36). Later, John used this reference for Jesus, as a Lamb, approximately twenty-four times in Revelation. Peter used the term once (1 Pet. 1:19). These writers recognized the reason for Jesus' death after the fact, but that was not an anticipated purpose of the Messiah, as recorded by prophesies of the Old Testament. One might even believe that Satan wasn't aware of this purpose, because if he had been, he would have done everything possible to prevent Jesus' crucifixion. Jesus clearly did understand, since it was the plan from the beginning. He gave hints to His disciples, but although they finally understood during the last week of His life that He would die in Jerusalem,[237] the concept of atonement was unclear to them, even after Jesus said early on, "Therefore My Father loves Me, because I lay down My life that I may take it again. No one takes it from Me, but I lay it down of Myself. I have power to lay it down, and I have power to take it again. This command I have received from My Father" (John 10:17–18, NKJV). The full consequences of Jesus' death do not appear to have been anticipated.

Why, then, were the leaders so angry at Him? Apparently, they were concerned about their own stature and position in society, and they didn't want to anger the Romans, even if they secretly hoped God would bring about their deliverance from them. Thus, the status quo was paramount to them. Jesus obviously did not rebel or violate any of God's laws. However, He did challenge the laws the Jewish establishment made, which placed unjustified rules and regulations upon the people. Those rules were merely religious rules that appeared right and enhanced the status of the leaders. They were not the rules that Adam, Noah, Abraham, or Moses were subjected to, yet those men were considered righteous by God. Because the Scriptures say that they were righteous, we can conclude they obeyed all of God's laws and made the appropriate atonement that was required when they failed to correctly follow the Law. They were considered righteous, but that does not mean they were sinless. Jesus, on the other hand, was sinless. He obeyed all of God's laws and lived by the spirit

---

236 See Isaiah 9:6–7; 35:5–6; 53:3–12; and 60:1–6. Many of these prophecies, and others, would only have been recognized after the fact. The religious leaders would not have known that Jesus fulfilled all of them. For example, how could they have known Jesus was born of a virgin, as indicated in Isaiah 7:14, and was named Immanuel.

237 See Matthew 17:23; 20:18–19; Mark 9:31; 10:33–34.

of the law. As such, when He was killed He became the perfect sacrifice for us, the final and only atonement available for our sin.

Many things angered the religious leaders at the time. This was because Jesus was not following the laws they judged to be necessary to be righteous. They also suffered wounded pride when they were chastised by someone who could do miracles and who was not a member of the "religious elite," one of their own. Finally, when Jesus said He was the Son of God, they could not tolerate the situation any longer. [238]

On top of the issue of their pride and what they believed to be blasphemy, oftentimes the religious authorities prohibited the miracles Jesus performed. In that period, many people believed in a correlation between sin and illness, so they didn't like Jesus healing people's infirmities because they felt that the sick deserved to be in their state (John 5:14; Mark 2:5; Luke 5:22–24). In at least one instance, Jesus said otherwise (John 9:2). One cannot accept an argument that the man was purposely made blind by God so that Jesus could heal him. Clearly that man had committed no sin prior to his birth. Thus, Jesus was breaking that connection that had formed in people's minds. Whether He was dealing with a physical problem or a psychosomatic/spiritual one, the people Jesus healed had tangible infirmities. In numerous accounts, He healed them immediately.

Potential Christians must confess their sins to Jesus and repent and change, all before their death. However, if you are saved, you should have no fear that you will have unrepentant sin that will keep you from the Father's presence. Please note that what some may perceive as a socially unacceptable activity does not necessarily constitute deadly or mortal sin and may not even be a sin by God's standard. You must seek the truth in God's Word and allow Him to deal with the condition of your heart. Is your heart greedy? Is it prideful? Are you willing to lie and distort the truth? Is love and mercy absent? It is true that pride can open itself to many different negative manifestations, including witchcraft, sexual immorality, and other satanic influences. However, this can be dealt with if you become aware of the situation and earnestly seek the Lord.

The baptism with the Holy Spirit is important, among other reasons, because

---

238 It is interesting that Jesus knew that this mixture of events would be the catalyst to cause His death before He created anything. Although the purpose is not mentioned in the Gospels, Jesus had Peter obtain some swords, though He never instructed the disciples to use them (John 18:11; Luke 22:36–38). Perhaps this was done so that the leaders could claim Jesus was leading an armed revolt. It is not recorded that they made the allegation, but Jesus did allude to it in Matthew 26:55.

it makes your spirit more sensitive and more responsive to the need for forgive-ness of sin. Note that there is no mention of your needing to perform any kind of penitence for the sin of which you have repented before your repentance is genuine. That is a matter of your heart. However, if you do not change, there is a limit on how many times you can ask forgiveness before you begin to trample on the Blood of Jesus. Paul indicated that at some point, not immediately after being saved and after experiencing the full gospel experience, one couldn't renew the experience of salvation because it would be like crucifying Jesus again (Heb. 6:4–6). What the benchmark or limit would be is not indicated.

?
11

MISCELLANEOUS FACTS AND CITATIONS

DID JESUS HAVE ANY BROTHERS OR SISTERS?

LUKE 2:7 SAYS Jesus was the firstborn of His mother, Mary (NIV, ASV, KJV, NKJV, NRSV, ISV). The King James Version and Darby's Translation also use this term in Matthew 1:25. The language of Matthew 1:25 indicates that Joseph had marital relations with Mary after Jesus was born.

Nonetheless, Roman Catholic and Eastern Orthodox churches believe that Mary remained a virgin. It is unclear if they only mean that in the sense that she bore no more children or that she had no sexual relations at all with Joseph.[239] Some might argue then that they were not married. According to Jewish Law, the purpose of marriage was to have children. If they did not have sexual relations, then they were not married. For those who believe that Mary remained a virgin, the more likely scenario would have to be that the statement in Matthew 1:25 is correct, but the brothers and sisters of Jesus were the children of Joseph from a previous marriage. Joseph does not appear to have been mentioned after Jesus was twelve years old. In addition, when Jesus was dying on the cross, He committed Mary to John, further evidence that Joseph was no longer alive to care for her. History indicates that Mary lived with John's family for approximately fifteen years.[240]

Luke received the information used as the basis for his Gospel from others. He may have even met some or all of Jesus' brothers and sisters, so his reference to Jesus being the firstborn may have been factually correct. On the other hand, he may have taken his verbiage from Matthew's Gospel, which predated his by approximately five years. Luke 8:19–21 references Jesus' mother and brothers coming to visit Him. (See also Mark 3:31; Matthew 12:46–47.) Mark

---

239 The underlying basis for this belief in the perpetual virginity of Mary appears to be that Mary is ascribed an elevated status by having no sexual relations with Joseph. This assumes that her primary value was being a vessel for Jesus.

240 Jamieson, Fausset, and Brown, s.v. "John 19."

6:3 and Matthew 13:55 mention them by name. They were James, Joseph, Judas, and Simon. Jesus' sisters are also mentioned, but not by name. Acts 1:14 also mentions brothers, this time after Jesus' ascension, and Paul mentions seeing James, the Lord's brother, in Galatians 1:19. James, often referred to as James the Just, became a leader in the early Christian church in Jerusalem and is generally credited with writing the Book of James in approximately A.D. 40–45. Jude stated he was a brother of James, rather than claiming to be Jesus' brother (Jude 1:11).

It appears to be clear that there were at least half-brothers and at least one half-sister. (See Mark 6:3; Matthew 13:56.) If all the brothers and sisters were only Joseph's, it could explain why none is mentioned as traveling to Jerusalem when Jesus was twelve years old. If any were more than twelve years younger than Jesus, born from the union between Joseph and Mary, Jesus probably would have inferred their existence when He spoke to John about taking care of Mary. It is unclear how Matthew would have inferred a sexual relationship between Joseph and Mary or that Jesus was the firstborn unless perhaps He had younger siblings. Then again, *firstborn* may just be a fourteenth century term, since not every Bible version uses that term. The American Standard, New International, and Revised Standard Versions do not use it. The King James and New King James Versions, as well as Young's Translation and the Darby New Testament, do use *firstborn*.

Thus, there could have been both children from Joseph's previous marriage and those siblings from Joseph's marriage to Mary. James was more than likely an older half-brother because, in all probability, for James to be a leader he had to be older. When Jesus assigned Mary into John's care, it could have been that the other children were established in their own family relationships. Since daughters often married very young, they could have been less than twenty years old at the time of Jesus' death but already married, which means they would not have been John's responsibility. Any other sons of Mary would probably still be at home, because of their age. The evidence is not conclusive one way or the other.

DID THE MAGI VISIT JESUS IN THE MANGER?

In Matthew 2:1–12, it is stated that after Jesus was born, Magi came to Jerusalem to find the one who had been born the King of the Jews. The shepherds had previously visited the stable while Jesus was in the manger, which was usually a wooden food trough used to feed animals in a stable. In Matthew 2:11, after Herod told the Magi where to find Jesus, the Magi found Jesus after Mary in a house. There is reason to believe it could have been more than a year after Jesus was born before the Magi visited Bethlehem. The time lapse between when the Magi saw the star appear and when they were talking with Herod is not indicated. Obviously, it was long enough for the Magi to decide to investigate and to travel to Jerusalem. This is also supported because Herod ordered all male children born in the previous two years to be killed (Matt. 2:16). If Herod had made his mandate only a matter of days after Jesus' birth, it is unlikely that he would have used a two-year period as a safety measure.

WHEN WAS JESUS BORN?

The winters, up to February, are mild in the region where Jesus was born. Therefore, it is possible that Jesus was born in either the December or January period. The best guess appears to be December 25, or January 6. He was born in approximately 4 to 6 B.C. Some, however, believe He was born in September.[241]

PRAYER IN GETHSEMANE

It is reported in Mark, Matthew, and Luke that Jesus prayed in Gethsemane, perhaps on the Mount of Olives, after the Last Supper (Mark 14:32–42; Matt. 26:36–46; Luke 22:39–46). Luke makes no mention of Jesus praying three times, but that is not significant. (Gospel writers of the same event will not note the same details.) Each of them recorded, although none of them was there, that Jesus asked that the cup, meaning the need for His upcoming death, be taken away if it was the Father's will. Matthew 26:37 states that Peter, James, and John went with Jesus, though John, who was there, does not mention the incident in his Gospel. Matthew, Mark, and Luke state that the three disciples with Jesus fell asleep, probably since He was praying for at least an hour (Matt. 26:40). Therefore, one has to wonder how they knew what Jesus prayed. This is especially true since James, Peter, and John were perhaps at least fifty or one hundred feet away from Jesus while He prayed.

However, perhaps the inconsistency about the prayer in Gethsemane is merely a misstatement regarding the timing. John mentions that while on the Mount of Olives during the last week but prior to the Last Supper, Jesus said, "Now My soul is troubled, and what shall I say? 'Father, save Me from this hour?' But for this purpose I came to this hour. Father, glorify Your name" (John 12:27–28). Of the Gospel writers, only John was present after the Last Supper, but all twelve disciples were present on the Mount of Olives before the

---

241 AllAboutJesusChrist.org, www.allaboutjesuschrist.org/was-jesus-born-on-december-25-faq.htm (accessed September 29, 2008).

Last Supper. Matthew, Mark, and Luke do not mention the event occurring except after the Last Supper and before Jesus was taken away.

Jesus knew before He created the world that He was going to be the ultimate sacrifice for a believer's sin. In fact, He had warned His disciples about His betrayal and death. Because of Jesus' statement in the Gospels about His soul being troubled over His coming crucifixion, some believe that there was a battle within Him about continuing His mission, though He submitted Himself to the Father's will.

If one believed that Jesus was merely a good human being, or another entity created by God, this view that He had an internal struggle, agonizing over the decision, might make sense. For example, Mormons believe that Jesus' atonement for man's sin began during this prayer.[242] They believe that Jesus shed His blood in the garden during His prayer. Luke is the only Gospel writer to mention that Jesus sweat to such an extent that the sweat drops were as large as blood drops, meaning the sweat was really running off Him. Even then, some of the ancient manuscripts do not have Luke 22:43–44. Those that rely on these verses to explain the atonement misunderstand them. Luke said "like blood," as nearly every translation states. If it were actual blood, he would have said Jesus sweat blood. Rather, the only place where His blood was shed was on the cross. Paul stated, "For God was pleased to have all his fullness dwell in him, and through him to reconcile to himself all things, whether things on earth or things in heaven, by making peace through his blood, shed on the cross" (Col. 1:19–20). The only mention of Jesus' shed blood is on the cross, predominately from His hands, feet, and side being pierced by a spear, which contributed to His death.[243]

Jesus, however, was more than an anointed, good human being. All the knowledge that He possessed before the Incarnation was still known to Him. The only possible gap would have been any changes that might have occurred in man's history while He had taken on flesh. Thus, perhaps Jesus was merely double-checking with the Father that nothing had occurred that would make His impending death pointless. Jesus would not have waivered in His commitment to the plan for man's salvation, which was put into motion when He

---

242 Mormons also believe the Atonement occurred on the cross as well as in the garden. Jesus was beaten, had a crown of thorns pushed into His head, and suffered spikes being driven into His flesh. All would have caused bleeding. For them, it is not the sacrificial death of Jesus that brings atonement, but the shedding of blood. (See www.lds.org.) However, the Atonement involves outside influences that caused the shedding of His blood, which was associated with His death.

243 People who were crucified died primarily of suffocation caused by the building up of carbon dioxide in the lungs, which resulted from an inability to take deep breaths because of constraints to their muscles. Breaking their legs hastened the process.

created everything. It would have been impossible for Jesus to back out at the last minute. He was God before birth, during His human life, and is still after His physical death and resurrection. It is not within His character to entertain the possibility of backing out, for He knew the importance of His sacrifice. Jesus would never succumb to any temptation to do anything that was counter to the original plan. He had already overcome Satan's temptations; why would He change His mind, considering all that He knew? Remember, Jesus said He was in the Father and the Father was in Him (John 14:11).

WHO WAS JUDAS?

Judas Iscariot was one of the original twelve disciples (Luke 22:14). He was sent out by Jesus to bring the message of the kingdom of God and demonstrate its power by healings and deliverance (Luke 9:1–2; Mark 6:7; Matt. 10:1–8). He was at the Last Supper when Jesus said that they, the disciples, would eat and drink at His table in His kingdom and rule the tribes of Israel from thrones (Luke 22:30). Notice that Judas was present even though Jesus knew before time was created that he would betray Him.

We know that Judas betrayed Jesus' location and identity when Jesus was being sought after by the religious leaders. There is no evidence that Judas expected Jesus to be executed. In fact, Judas repented of his role in Jesus' death, which he called a betrayal of "innocent blood," and hanged himself when he heard Jesus had been condemned by the Jewish religious authorities (Matt. 27:3–5). We will never know Judas' reasons for turning Jesus in. However, it is clear that he knew Jesus' power and authority. Apparently, however, he did not grasp the fact that there was a long-term, worldwide reason for Jesus' time on Earth and that His death was an essential part of the plan for man's salvation. After Judas's death, he was replaced by Matthias after lots were cast to determine who would take his place.[244] Both Matthias and the other candidate, Joseph, who was apparently called Barsabbas, were undoubtedly two of the Seventy sent out by Jesus (Luke 10:1). The essential criterion for selection was that they had been with the apostles throughout Jesus' ministry (Acts 1:22).

Will Judas still rule the tribes of Israel from heaven? Luke said Judas went to his own place, but the meaning is unclear (Acts 1:25). The New International

---

244 The use of lots or the casting of lots was used for centuries and recorded several times in the Old Testament. It was usually done so that no one could later claim the choice had been fixed or controlled by undisclosed reasons. In this case, however, the other apostles prayed to God that He would control the outcome. The actual materials used in biblical times are not really known with certainty, but the concept of casting lots is well known today, though by a different term: casting dice.

Version records that Jesus said that none of the disciples were lost "except the one doomed to destruction" (John 17:12); many other translations do not employ this word in describing Judas's fate. Several other versions use the term *son of perdition* (NKJV, DNT, KJV). Merriam-Webster's dictionary defines *perdition* as "eternal damnation," or hell.[245]

WHEN DID JESUS DIE?

When Jesus was alive, the Julian calendar was being used. The Julian calendar had errors in it, and the Gregorian calendar replaced it in approximately 1580.[246] Because of the differences in these two systems, the date could be off by several years.

It is unknown exactly how old He was, but since He probably reached between thirty-three and thirty-eight years of age, it is very likely that He died either in A.D. 30 or 33. (In our calendar, A.D. 1 follows after 1 B.C.) Astronomical studies and correlation with the Jewish calendar regarding the celebration of the Passover support either A.D. 30 or 33 as the year of Jesus' death. However, the reference in John 2:20 to the time of the temple construction means Jesus' ministry could have started as early as approximately A.D. 27. This, too, lends strong support to the theory that Jesus died in A.D. 30.[247]

WHEN IS EASTER?

Easter is on the first Sunday after the full moon on or after March 21.

WHAT HAPPENED TO THE APOSTLES?

There are few accurate accounts of the apostles, where they preached the gospel, and how they died. Where they preached is often only known because of legends and traditions handed down from the original churches. The following tables give you a general sense of where they traveled, how they died, and what books of the Bible many of them wrote.

245　*Merriam-Webster's Collegiate Dictionary, 11th edition* (Springfield, MA: Merriam-Webster, Inc., 2003), s.v. "perdition."

246　See en.Wikipedia.org/wiki/julian_calendar and en.Wikipedia.org/wiki/Gregorian_calendar (accessed September 29, 2008).

247　A. T. Robertson, *A Harmony of the Gospels* (New York, NY: HarperOne, 1932); and Robert L. Thomas, Stanley N. Gundry, *The NIV Harmony of the Gospels* (New York, NY: Harper Collins, 1988).

WHERE THEY TRAVELED AND HOW THEY DIED[248]

Name	Area of Ministry	Year and Method of Death
Peter	Israel, Italy	67—crucified upside down
Andrew	Greece, Russia	Crucified
John	Turkey	98–100—natural causes
James	Israel	44—beheaded
Matthew	Persia, Ethiopia	60—stabbed
Thomas	India, China	Stabbed
Phillip	Carthage	Crucified
Bartholomew	Arabia, Ethiopia, India	Crucified
James (Alphaeus)	Syria	66—stoned
Thaddeus	Greece	72—crucified
Simon (Canaanite)	Britain, Europe	Crucified
Judas Iscariot		Hanged himself
Matthias	Syria	Burned to death
Paul (Saul)	Israel, Greece, Italy	67—beheaded

A CHRONOLOGY OF THE NEW TESTAMENT BOOKS[249]

Book	Author	Date Written
Matthew	Matthew	60–63
Mark	John Mark	60–63
Luke	Luke	63–65
John	John	85–90
Acts	Luke	61–66
Romans	Paul	56–58
1 Corinthians	Paul	54–56
2 Corinthians	Paul	55–57
Galatians	Paul	49–52
Ephesians	Paul	60–62

---

248 The years of death listed are approximate due to differences in the Julian and Gregorian calendars, and some of the areas of ministry may be wrong, such as in the case of Simon the Canaanite. Part of the error may also be caused by the fact that the apostles and some of the early church leaders were called by the same name.

249 Note that Paul's letters are not placed in the Bible in chronological order.

Book	Author	Date Written
Philippians	Paul	62–63
Colossians	Paul	60–61
1 Thessalonians	Paul	50–52
2 Thessalonians	Paul	52–53
1 Timothy	Paul	62–64
2 Timothy	Paul	65–67
Titus	Paul	62–64
Philemon	Paul	60–61
Hebrews	attributed to Paul	64–65
James	James	45
1 Peter	Peter	63–64
2 Peter	Peter	63–64
1 John	John	80–90
2 John	John	80–90
3 John	John	80–90
Jude	Jude	67–68
Revelation	John	90–95

12

CULTS

THOSE THAT PRETEND TO BE CHRISTIAN

CULTS HAVE A common trait: their beliefs are based upon the writings or revelation of an individual or group.[250] These cult writings are often elevated to a level equal to or even higher than the Bible, although they often will claim they are merely explaining or revealing hidden truths in the Bible. Usually, though, these hidden truths are simply fanciful speculations or fantasy whose purpose is to lift up the cult leadership in order to allow them to extend their control over their followers. Some such leaders will even publish their own Bible, such as the Jehovah's Witnesses' New World Translation and the Latter Day Saints' Inspired Version. They claim that they have done so because there is a need to use more contemporary English, but they use it as an opportunity to change words to support their doctrines. If an organization uses its own publication as justification to support its position on important topics such as the Trinity, it is probably a cult. True Christian churches are not based on a single individual's interpretation of the Word or on non-standard Bibles.

Another warning indicator that you are in a cult is if the religious organization establishes a set of rules that, when followed, grants you a level of privilege not available to everyone. An organization that has different classes or rankings for its members feeds people's pride by placing an emphasis on works, not faith. It does not honor God if those who meet the qualifications for the higher ranking—even if it is supposedly because they are pleasing God—are considered more dedicated than those who fail. When there is a lack of openness and equality for all members before God, it is not of Him.

A third indicator is if the religious organization places a major emphasis on good works, even though they are merely works of the flesh. Beware if they are

---

250 Claiming to have more than one source is no guarantee that the material they espouse is true and that their religious system is not a cult.

very dedicated to performing good works and measuring their righteousness by them.

Sometimes even those who believe they are Christian promote allegedly new doctrines. One example is the belief being taught in some churches now that since Jesus died for all, all will be saved. They teach that those who are not saved during this life will be given another opportunity after their death. However, there is no place in the Scriptures that states the decision to follow Jesus may be made after death. To propose that idea is not only speculative, but it would be counter to what Jesus clearly said in many instances, including John 5:28–29 (NKJV):

> Do not marvel at this; for the hour is coming in which all who are in the graves will hear His voice and come forth—those who have done good, to the resurrection of life, and those who have done evil, to the resurrection of condemnation.

Furthermore, John the Baptist said, "He who believes in the Son has everlasting life; and he who does not believe the Son shall not see life, but the wrath of God abides on him" (John 2:36, NKJV). In Matthew 10:32–33 (NKJV), Jesus said, "Therefore whoever confesses Me before men, him I will also confess before My Father who is in heaven. But whoever denies Me before men, him I will also deny before My Father who is in heaven." Jesus also warned, "Because narrow is the gate and difficult is the way which leads to life, and there are few who find it" (Matt. 7:14, NKJV). Thus, although Jesus died for all, He said that not all would be saved, yet if posthumous decisions to believe in Christ were permissible, who, standing before Jesus in eternity, would not make the choice to believe in Him?

Seeking God through the Old Testament scriptures is not a valid substitute for salvation through Christ. This is just another type of denial of Him. For example, Jesus, in reference to the Jews, said in John 5:39–40 (NKJV), "You search the Scriptures, for in them you think you have eternal life; and these are they which testify of Me. But you are not willing to come to Me that you may have life."

Jesus also said, "For my Father's will is that everyone who looks to the Son and believes in him shall have eternal life, and I will raise him up at the last day" (John 6:40); and, "I tell you the truth, he who believes has everlasting life" (John 6:47). Thus, Jesus came for all, but only those who believe in Him while they are alive will have everlasting life. You must accept Christ Jesus as your Savior while you are alive. If you do not, you will die a sinner, and there is no second chance after death.

MORMONS: THE CHURCH OF JESUS CHRIST OF LATTER-DAY SAINTS

Mormons believe that everyone is really a spirit created by God and that Jesus is higher than the angels, but all will eventually be in heaven. This idea has been around for at least 1,500 years. In fact, this is an offshoot of Gnostic teachings, which attacked the divinity of Jesus. There are so many false beliefs and doctrines in this cult that have no biblical or even a logical basis that they cannot all be adequately addressed in this book.

Sadly, they have used man's need for love to create a community that is in bondage to the demonic spirits of Satan. This evil is compounded by their use of the name of Jesus, even though it is not the same Jesus represented in the Gospels. Thus, many people are deceived by their words into believing they are Christian. Many Mormons represent themselves to be—and truly believe they are—part of the true church of Jesus, when they are just the opposite.[251]

Belief About Christianity	Position
Trinity (pre-incarnate Jesus)	No
Jesus	Created by God, higher than angels
Resurrection	No
Virgin Birth	Not as the Bible teaches

JEHOVAH'S WITNESSES

The Jehovah's Witnesses believe they are the only true church[252] and that only 144,000 will make it to heaven with the rest of the saved, who will live on an earthly paradise after the millennial reign of Christ. They do not believe in the Holy Spirit, except as a "force." Jehovah's Witnesses even have their own translation of the Bible, the New World Translation. In it they have changed the wording to diminish the divinity of Jesus. For example, in John 17:5, all major Bibles say something similar to, "Father, glorify me in your presence with the glory I had with you before the world began." The New World Translation says, "Father, glorify me alongside yourself with the glory that I had alongside you

---

251 For more information on Mormons and their history, see *Under the Banner of Heaven* by Jon Krakauer (Doubleday, 2003).

252 There is no single group that makes up the true church. The true church is comprised of individuals from various Christian denominations whose Head is Jesus.

before the world was."[253] Thus, Jesus is separated from God, not part of God. They also do not believe Jesus had the power to resurrect Himself, which contradicts John 10:18. They also misstate John 1:1–2 as follows, "In [the] beginning the Word was, and the Word was with God, and the Word was a god. This one was in [the] beginning with God." Notice the small g on the word *god*. Mainline Christian Bibles say, "In the beginning was the Word, and the Word was with God, and the Word was God. He was with God in the beginning."

Belief About Christianity	Position
Trinity (pre-incarnate Jesus)	No
Jesus	Created by God, then used by God in creation
Resurrection	No
Virgin Birth	No

THE CHURCH OF CHRIST, SCIENTIST: THE CHRISTIAN SCIENCE CHURCH

They believe strongly in healing by prayer. Consulting medical science for healing is not prohibited, but it is discouraged. They do not believe in evil and tend to circumvent both the major Christian doctrine of the Trinity and the belief that Jesus died as the only atonement for our sin. Thus, Jesus is a means to an end, and there is no relationship with Him. Suffering is because of sin, but not even His death may atone for it. They have misconceptions on the meaning of faith and hold to a variety of other false concepts, such as the following:

- Heaven and hell are merely states of mind and not part of an afterlife.
- Jesus embodied the divinity of God, but He was not Deity.
- Adherents are taught to follow the ministry of Jesus—that is, do what He said to do—but they reject who He was. For example, they appear to believe that sin is a matter of belief, and belief in sin is punished. They acknowledge God's forgiveness of sin, but appear to believe that evil is cast out of us. While they acknowledge Jesus' atonement, they do not understand it to be the only sacrifice for sin. Our unity with God is through Jesus, but the reality of God's ultimate love sacrifice, His death, is rejected.[254]

253 The New World Translation of the Holy Scriptures (New York, NY: Watchtower Society, 1950).

254 See www.ChristianScience.com (accessed September 29, 2008).

Belief About Christianity	Position
Trinity (pre-incarnate Jesus)	No
Jesus	The spiritual idea of God
Resurrection	Yes
Virgin Birth	Yes

SEVENTH-DAY ADVENTISM

While accepted as Christian by many, they blend Old Testament legal concepts into their beliefs, yielding a mixture of the Law and salvation by faith. Services are held on Saturday in accordance with the Old Testament, which seems to be at odds with what Jesus said in Luke 5:36–39. Many of their beliefs are merely conjecture about ideas not expressed in the New Testament.

Belief About Christianity	Position
Trinity (pre-incarnate Jesus)	Yes
Jesus	Yes
Resurrection	Yes
Virgin Birth	Yes

CHRISTIAN UNIVERSALISM

Christian universalists have learned over the last two hundred years to use Christian terminology to pass themselves off as a Christian organization. They claim they believe in Jesus and the Trinity. Their message is deceptive and beguiling in that it professes many Christian principles while ignoring any need for a personal faith in and relationship with Jesus while we are alive. They profess that a relationship with Jesus is unnecessary since Jesus died for all, a belief which comes from their interpretation of 1 Timothy 2:4 (KJV): "Who will have all men to be saved, and to come unto the knowledge of the truth."

Their position, which has been circulating since approximately 1800, is that all of mankind will ultimately be saved through Jesus, whether or not any faith is involved on man's part while they are alive.[255] In other words, they believe man is automatically saved because of God's love and justice, which is taken to mean that eternal punishment, or hell, is a false doctrine based upon an alleged misinterpretation of certain Greek words in the Bible. They do believe that there will be punishment for sins in an afterlife, but that the punishment

---

255 See Thomas Whittmore's *Plain Guide to Universalism*, which was originally published in 1840.

is remedial in nature and designed to cause man to change into a righteous being. Hell, according to their concept of it, is a temporary site in which men who have not experienced salvation while alive will have their sins purged and will be saved and transformed into the image of Jesus. They totally reject the concept of eternal torment, even though Matthew 25:41 says in several translations that the fire of hell is everlasting and eternal. They also conclude that if every knee shall bow before Jesus and "every tongue confess that Jesus Christ is Lord, to the glory of God the Father" (Phil. 2:10–11), this event must occur after judgment, perhaps after being changed by the purifying fire (as opposed to before judgment).

A more clear meaning of 1 Timothy 2:4 is that God would like or desire all men to be saved, not that all men will be saved. Paul did not say all men are or will be saved, merely that Jesus died for all men. Jesus clearly indicated that not all men will be saved, for He said in Matthew 25:41, "Then he will say to those on his left, 'Get away from me, you who are accursed, into the eternal fire that has been prepared for the devil and his angels!'" (ISV). He may not have used the term *hell* in this passage, but the implications are clear that He was referring to *hell*, or the lake of burning fire and brimstone, for a second death (Rev. 21:8; Luke 12:5). Jesus clearly indicated that being cast into hell, with its fire, was something to avoid (Matt. 5:22; 18:9) Jesus said in Luke 13:23–28 (NKJV):

> Then one said to Him, "Lord, are there few who are saved?" And He said to them, "Strive to enter through the narrow gate, for many, I say to you, will seek to enter and will not be able. When once the Master of the house has risen up and shut the door, and you begin to stand outside and knock at the door, saying, 'Lord, Lord, open for us,' and He will answer and say to you, 'I do not know you, where you are from,' then you will begin to say, 'We ate and drank in Your presence, and You taught in our streets.' But He will say, 'I tell you I do not know you, where you are from. Depart from Me, all you workers of iniquity.' There will be weeping and gnashing of teeth, when you see Abraham and Isaac and Jacob and all the prophets in the kingdom of God, and yourselves thrust out."

Because they believe a loving God would not have anyone lost, they cannot accept the idea that the consequences for those who have never heard of Jesus would be any different from those who have made Him their Lord. The net effect of their belief is to make Jesus merely one option—among many others—to be accepted by God. To judge God by man's idea of love and justice is a grave error, tantamount to rebellion against God and His plan of salvation. His plan existed before creation and it does not have alternatives.

Paul wrote in Romans about people who have not had any opportunity to hear about Jesus and explained that they are not above judgment because the knowledge of God is made plain to all men in creation (Rom. 1:18–20). In addition, Jesus indicated that following the Old Testament but denying Christ as one's Savior will not bring eternal life (John 5:39–40). Rejection of this principle brings judgment (John 12:48). Thus, it appears that all will be held accountable. If someone does not come to believe in Him, he or she will be treated as if they rejected Him. Can anyone refuse to seek the truth, particularly considering the availability of information today, and then claim ignorance at the time of judgment? Jesus said, "He who believes and is baptized will be saved; but he who does not believe will be condemned" (Mark 16:16). We can no more decide to believe in Jesus after we die than we can to be baptized with water in the afterlife.

The question that Christian universalists should ask themselves is why man was created. Their remedy for sinful man, one that doesn't require faith, could just as easily have been applied to the fallen angels, without the need for the creation of Man. The fact that Man was created must mean that the use of punishment, or perhaps it should be called "spirit modification" to conform an angel's character into an acceptable quality or form, is not God's plan. Consequently, since there is no second chance for salvation, after our death, there must be a permanent separation from God, for sinners.

CONCLUSION

BEFORE TIME WAS created, God desired to share Himself with a creation that would love and trust Him above all else. In order for that to occur, His creation had to be allowed to have the free will to decide for itself whether it desired to be with God or to promote its own self-interest. To prove that love, trust, and faith in God were preferable to any other choices available, He created spirit beings called angels. They had free will, but some decided that they were more interested in their own self-will and challenged God. God cast them from His presence, but He also, as He had planned from the beginning, created a world and man.

Man was also given the right to exercise free will, but he was given a few rules to follow. As expected, man failed to honor God in his exercise of free will. Man, over the centuries, proved to be very poor at following rules. Then again, that was part of the point of the rules. Rules don't create faith, they inhibit it. Rules only influence man's choices, and when we chose to follow them, it is to avoid undesired consequences, gain rewards, or to feel prideful. As part of God's plan, He knew that man's spirit needed to be reborn and changed into His likeness—and that this could only occur through faith in Him.

The Son of God, a part of the Trinity, came and took on the limitations of flesh by being born of a woman. This was Jesus. His purpose was to be the perfect sacrifice for man's sin, which allowed man to have his spirit reborn, free of sin. This rebirth usually begins with a mental acceptance or belief. However, the fact that Jesus, the Son of God, died for us and was resurrected to life, must reach the level of faith within one's heart.

This initial experience of faith leads to our salvation. However, changing into the spiritual likeness of Jesus only starts with salvation. It is the door we spiritually go through, but there is a path on the other side. This path includes the sanctification process.

What, then, is our goal as Christians? It should be to change, as much as we can, into the likeness of Jesus. We will never completely achieve that goal during our lifetime, but we should try to take on His attributes. In order for that to become possible, we must first understand who Jesus is and why He came to be the only acceptable sacrifice for our sins. Because of His sacrifice, there is no other option under which man can become united with God in everlasting life, except by first having the Spirit of Christ come into our heart (Gal. 4:6).

Once that concept is understood, it becomes important for us to change from our old ways and the ways of the world into the likeness of Jesus. How is this achieved? It does not involve acts of disciplining our flesh under a set of prescribed laws or even by doing religious activities, but instead it involves the changing of our spirit. This change is known as the sanctification process, a process of spiritual change in which God manifests His Spirit in us as we become more like Him.

In John 17:17–21 (NKJV), Jesus said, "Sanctify them by Your truth. Your word is truth. As You sent Me into the world, I also have sent them into the world. And for their sakes I sanctify Myself, that they also may be sanctified by the truth. I do not pray for these alone, but also for those who will believe in Me through their word; that they all may be one, as You, Father, are in Me, and I in You; that they also may be one in Us, that the world may believe that You sent Me."

At the time of salvation, we begin the process by being sanctified by the blood of Jesus (Heb. 13:12). In other words, our spirit is cleansed of repentant sin, but the character or our spirit is as yet unchanged. Further, as the bride of Christ, His church, we are further sanctified by the washing of the Word (Eph. 5:26). This process, however, is only partially accomplished by the reading of the Word. It is heavily dependent on prayer and time in the presence of the Lord. Paul said in Ephesians 4:23–24, "And be renewed in the spirit of your mind, and that you put on the new man which was created according to God, in true righteousness and holiness" (NKJV). This requires a sensitive spirit that can hear the Holy Spirit when He attempts to influence our spirit, not just our minds.

For example, in Romans 8:26–27 Paul said, "Likewise the Spirit also helps in our weaknesses. For we do not know what we should pray for as we ought, but the Spirit Himself makes intercession for us with groanings which cannot be uttered. Now He who searches the hearts knows what the mind of the Spirit is, because He makes intercession for the saints according to the will of God" (NKJV). Paul also said in 1 Corinthians 2:10–12, "But God has revealed them to us through His Spirit. For the Spirit searches all things, yes, the deep things of God....Even so no one knows the things of God except the Spirit of God.

Now we have received, not the spirit of the world, but the Spirit who is from God, that we might know the things that have been freely given to us by God" (NKJV). In this regard, Paul said we should pray for the wisdom and revelation that is produced by His Spirit within us. Further, in Ephesians 1:17 Paul said, "The God of our Lord Jesus Christ, the Father of glory, may give to you the spirit of wisdom and revelation in the knowledge of Him" (NKJV).

With this access to the Holy Spirit's influence on our spirit, Paul's statement in 2 Corinthians 7:1 is understood: "Therefore, having these promises, beloved, let us cleanse ourselves from all filthiness of the flesh and spirit, perfecting holiness in the fear of God" (NKJV). While we only begin the process of changing our spirit through prayer, we also need to reflect the changes in our spirit in our daily life. For example, in Galatians 5:16–18 Paul said, "I say then: Walk in the spirit, and you shall not fulfill the lust of the flesh. For the flesh lusts against the Spirit, and the Spirit against the flesh; and these are contrary to one another, so that you do not do the things that you wish. But if you are led by the Spirit, you are not under the law" (NKJV).

The entire sanctification process is greatly assisted and facilitated by the baptism with the Holy Spirit. It is also the process whereby our spirit is cleansed from evil influences so that we can discern good from evil. Along the way, we must also be able to discern false doctrines and false groups that claim to be Christian. The apostle John said in 1 John 4:1, "Beloved, do not believe every spirit, but test the spirits, whether they are of God; because many false prophets have gone out into the world" (NKJV). This book has explained some of these issues so that you will gain wisdom and maturity so that "then [you] will no longer be little children, tossed like waves and blown about by every wind of doctrine, by people's trickery, or by clever strategies that would lead [you] astray" (Eph. 4:14, ISV).

TO CONTACT THE AUTHOR
Al.Hall@charter.net